A Manager's Guide to Sexual Orientation in the Workplace

Bob Powers and Alan Ellis

Routledge   New York and London

Published in 1995 by
Routledge
29 West 35th Street
New York, NY 10001

Published in Great Britain by
Routledge
11 New Fetter Lane
London EC4P 4EE

Library of Congress Cataloging-in-Publication Data

Powers, Bob, 1941—
     A manager's guide to sexual orientation in the workplace / Bob Powers
and Alan Ellis.
     p.   cm.
     Includes bibliographical references.
     ISBN 0-415-91277-6
     1. Gays—Employment.   2. Lesbians—Employment.   3. Sexual orientation.
4. Executives—Attitudes.   5. Diversity in the workplace.   6. Gays—Case
studies.   7. Lesbians—Case studies.   I. Ellis, Alan, 1957— .   II. Title.

HD6285.P69   1995   95-23654
658.3'045—dc20   CIP

Praise for

A Manager's Guide to Sexual Orientation in the Workplace:

▼

*Not only does A **Manager's Guide** show why sexual orientation, like all diversity, is a business issue, it shows how it affects total performance and gives managers the tools and resources to dramatically improve performance. This is a powerful book!*

> —Mike Underhill, Diversity Consultant,
> Amoco Corporation

In today's global, competitive world, no company can afford to get less than the best from all its employees. Bob Powers' new work provides valuable insights and practical advice for managers on how they, their staffs, and their companies can do better by being better.

> —Elliot Maxwell, Director, International
> Technology Policy, Department of Commerce

*Written expressly for heterosexuals, this book equips managers to tackle the toughest of all diversity issues— sexual orientation. A **Manager's Guide** is much needed!*

> —Julie O'Mara, Author of **Managing Workforce 2000** and past President, American Society for Training and Development

A Manager's Guide to Sexual Orientation in the Workplace

This book is dedicated to Robert Wood, who helped me to "come out" and introduced me to the "gay underground" at AT&T

—Bob Powers

and to Colin Van Uchelen and Mindy Mechanic—two caring heterosexuals—who supported me in the early stages of my "coming out" at the University of Illinois.

—Alan Ellis

Contents

Acknowledgments

There are many people we would like to thank for their support in developing this guide, most especially the authors of the eleven life stories. Without their courageous and remarkable portraits, this guide simply wouldn't exist. So our hats are off to Dale Barr, Lisa Busjahn, Luann Conaty, Frederick Hewitt-Cruz, Constance Holmes, Mick Miller, Art Moreno, Vince Patton, Jillaine Smith, Joe Wilcox, and Frank Wong. The world's corporations will be enriched by your efforts.

In addition, we would like to thank Dennis De Biase for introducing us to our wonderful editor, Cecelia Cancellaro. Cecelia, along with Paul Williams of Routledge, saw the promise of this book. We also want to thank Laurie Harper of the Sebastian Agency for her hard work and encouragement, the staff at A Different Light for the access to resources they provided, and the many others who have helped us along the way, including Roger Addison, Dr. David Berensen, Bill Coscarelli, Vanessa Inn, Julie O'Mara, James Robertson, and Ayo Yetunde.

Bob Powers   Alan Ellis

Getting Oriented

1

Knowledge, Skills, and Resources

Ignorance may be bliss in some settings, but in the corporate world, ignorance, or a lack of knowledge, is one of the two prime reasons organizations fail (see the *Handbook of Human Performance Technology*, 1992, Jossey-Bass, San Francisco). And managers lack knowledge about the impact of sexual orientation on workplace performance. *Fortune* magazine, in its December 1991 cover story entitled "Gay in Corporate America," said that even most educated people are misinformed about gay and lesbian issues.

What is the second primary reason organizations fail? The answer is a lack of execution. In other words, people *know* what to do, but they *don't* do it because they lack the skills and resources required to perform successfully.

When people lack knowledge, skills, or resources, productivity suffers. Unless you are well-educated on the issues of sexual orientation and their impact on workplace performance *and* possess the skills and resources required to effectively manage these issues, you will not get optimal performance from the employees within your organization. *A Manager's Guide to Sexual Orientation in the Workplace* will provide you with the tools you need to effectively manage these issues and attain top-notch performance from all of your employees.

SEXUAL MINORITIES: A NEW WORLD OF VISIBILITY

No one really knows for sure how widespread homosexuality is, but most studies suggest between three percent and ten percent of the population, and thus the workforce, is gay. Even three percent is a hefty number for most organizations. If you apply these percentages to your customer base, you are looking at BIG numbers.

From Apple to Xerox, the world's top corporations are beginning to recognize and address this large base of employees and customers. And why not? According to the workbook, *Sexual Orientation in the Workplace* (1994, International Partners Press, Santa Cruz), the gay, lesbian, and bisexual customer base has a combined income of more than $500 billion. And, in a January 24, 1993 article, the *San Francisco Chronicle* reported that there are 25 million gay and lesbian customers in the United States alone, and they possess a median annual household income of $42,000 for gay men and $39,000 for lesbians. With numbers such as these, and the opportunities they present, why has it taken so long for American firms to wake up to this abundant market? The answers are obvious. The issues of sexuality (in general) and variations from heterosexuality (in particular) are controversial, and until recently, most gay, lesbian, and bisexual employees and customers lived quiet, even closeted, corporate lives. In effect, these sexual minorities remained invisible, perpetuating a myth that purports "they don't exist in our company." Today, most everyone recognizes that sexual minorities do exist and that they no longer are content to remain closeted or quiet.

> [D]own in the trenches at many companies, unfamiliar lifestyles are being demystified at lunch, over coffee and in meetings. Mere familiarity begins to change perceptions. "Until recently, most Americans couldn't say the words 'gay' or 'lesbian' without thinking that something weird was coming out of their mouths," said Bob Powers, a diversity consultant in San Francisco
>
> —*New York Times*, June 13, 1993.

As sexual minorities step out of their corporate closets, heterosexuals begin to ask questions. Thousands of heterosexuals ask us the same questions over and over again: "When did you choose to be gay?" and "Why do you have to flaunt it?" If the first question didn't have such serious implications, most of us (gay people) would laugh hysterically at just hearing the question. Who on earth would choose an orientation for which you are guaranteed to be laughed at, lied about, hated, insulted, probably ostracized from your family, physically abused, and quite possibly lose your children and even your life? And if you're not killed by someone else, you might do it yourself—like the 30% of all teen-agers who commit suicide because they are gay or lesbian and unable to cope in a homophobic world.

When asked, "When did you choose to be gay?" we respond, as in the following (typical) dialogue, by asking a series of questions:

Are you heterosexual?
Yes.
When did you choose to be a heterosexual?
What do you mean?
I mean, when did you choose to be a heterosexual?
I didn't choose to be a heterosexual.
You didn't?
No.
You mean you just are a heterosexual?
Yes.
Well, we just are homosexuals.
Oh, I didn't realize it was the same for you.

Generally, at that moment the questioner *realizes* that our sexual orientation is no more a choice than the color of our skin, the curl of our hair, or the size of our heart.

When asked, "Why do you have to flaunt it?" we generally respond that if we don't "flaunt it" we will forever remain invisible, responsible for contributing to the myth that "we don't exist."

Besides, we add, heterosexuals "flaunt" their sexuality all the time. Generally, this notion comes as a surprise to most heterosexuals. "We don't flaunt our sexuality," they protest over and over again. Yet, any gay person can tell you that most heterosexuals mention their husband or wife or their children or talk about family events such as weddings, honeymoons, anniversaries, births, and divorces within the first few minutes of meeting them. They are quick to flash pictures of their kids and spouses or show off engagement rings, wedding rings, or other symbols generally considered heterosexual. And you know what? There is nothing wrong with flaunting sexual orientation. It's simply human nature, a matter of stating, "This is who I am." Each of us has this right whether we're heterosexual, homosexual, bisexual, or transsexual.

Most of us were brought up to avoid discussions of sexuality, and especially homosexuality. This makes the new visibility of sexual minorities—of people who are different—difficult for many to accept. If you wonder about this, recall the first time you saw someone in a wheelchair. If your parents were like many, they said to you within a matter of seconds, "Don't stare." The message was clear. Avoid people in wheelchairs, men in turbans, women wearing veils, street people, flamboyant people, anybody, in fact, who is *different from you*.

When people are expected to be invisible—as sexual minorities are—they tend to act in extreme ways. They either go into hiding (pretending to be someone they are not) or they "act up," (protesting, disrupting). Neither response is the most effective way to improve productivity or work relations, nor do they allow people to be themselves at work.

THE LINK BETWEEN SEXUAL ORIENTATION AND PERFORMANCE

A high-level manager recently asked, "Does sexual orientation impact performance?" That's a good question and, surprisingly, the answer is absolutely! When managers send signals or messages that it is not okay to be gay in the workplace, and they do, they negatively impact performance. Some managers send blatant signals such as making statements like, "Who do you people think you are talking about your sexual orientation in public?" or "We don't want any of them in here." More often, the messages are subtle, such as, "Gays and lesbians are okay so long as they don't talk about it." Whether blatant or subtle, the messages are the same to sexual minorities—you can't be yourself here—and when people are made to feel unwelcome, their performance is negatively impacted. If heterosexual employees were made to feel that their sexual orientation was not okay, their performance would suffer also.

When negative messages or signals are sent, many employees feel forced to hide their sexual identity. This hiding takes a tremendous amount of psychological and physical energy. These employees divert their energies away from work performance to protect themselves by covering up facts, keeping low profiles, lying, changing pronouns, and so forth. Anyone who has ever hid a significant part of their life can understand the energy hiding takes— the boss who is hiding a diagnosis of cancer, an employee who is hiding that her son is dying of AIDS, two employees who are hiding their intimate relationship, or a coworker who is hiding an addiction.

While most people understand that hiding wastes energy, they often continue (both knowingly and unknowingly) to send signals and messages that encourage people to hide.

Whenever a manager or coworker tells a homophobic, racist, or sexist joke, the message is sent that it is not okay to be yourself. Every time we exclude sexual minorities, we reinforce the message that sexual minorities are not welcome. Often this is done inadvertently—for example, in training classes where role plays contain references only to opposite sex couples or in invitations to office parties in which husbands and wives are encouraged to attend but no attempt is made to include same-sex partners. Although seemingly subtle, these acts reinforce the message that one needs to hide simply to survive.

When people feel excluded, as sexual minorities often do, they are much less inclined to devote energy toward making the organization successful. Ask yourself how likely you would be to go out of your way to help an organization that tells you there is something wrong with who you are, that says, in effect, "you're not welcome." The answer is, "not very likely."

> If you are heterosexual and have any doubts about the effort it takes to hide, try this simple experiment for a day or even during a fifteen minute coffee break. Go the entire time without making a single reference to your spouse, children, family, or significant other or making any other statement that would give even a hint of your heterosexuality. In trying to hide your sexual orientation, you will experience the difficulty that sexual minorities face. It becomes almost impossible to answer even the most

> simple questions. Questions like, "What did you do over the weekend?" "What are you planning to do tonight?" "Do you have a family or a partner?" Most people cannot go two minutes without revealing their sexual orientation. And those who resort to hiding who they are end up feeling dishonest, powerless, and often disgusted with themselves, traits not especially conducive to improving workplace performance.

Another response people have to being made invisible is to "act up" or "act out" rather than hide. Forcing people to be invisible has led disabled people to wheel in protest down America's main streets, AIDS activists to shout down Presidents, women to break through the doors of the U.S. Senate, and people of every color to march arm-in-arm through towns and villages around the world, from Selma, Alabama, to Johannesburg, South Africa. And, it has led gays, lesbians, and other sexual minorities to stand up and shout out, "We're here! We're queer! Get used to it!" Not only can you get used to it, you can also come to enjoy and find value in embracing this diverse group of coworkers, employees, bosses, and customers.

The 25 million U.S. gay and lesbian customers are a group of knowledgeable consumers. They are also a group to quickly spread word throughout the sexual minority community about companies that have homophobic practices and policies. They are well organized to boycott homophobic firms and fiercely loyal to companies with a history of acceptance and outreach to the community. Your actions as a manager represent your company and directly link to the bottom line, so it makes sense to ask yourself, "How do I manage?"

HOW DO I MANAGE?

How do you know if you are managing in a way that makes people feel welcomed and included? How do you know if the signals and messages that you send tell people to hide, to be invisible, in effect, to be unproductive?

Let's look at some of the things that can help you decide how you manage. First, when it comes to these issues, there are basically three groups of managers. Check the group which best represents you.

1 I am blatantly homophobic and discriminatory.
2 I am not blatantly homophobic but I prefer not to talk about these issues at work.
3 I am welcoming and inclusive and I freely talk about these issues with my colleagues, superiors, and subordinates.

If you checked the first group, let us commend you for reading this book. You are taking a step in the right direction. Frankly, we don't expect too many readers to be in this group.

If you checked group two, and we suspect many of you did, it's unlikely you're getting the kind of performance possible from your employees, especially those who consider themselves as part of a sexual minority or simply different from you. Not talking about these issues is a form of denial and, inadvertently, sends signals that it is not okay for employees to be themselves, which results in a loss of performance. You need to find a way that makes it relatively comfortable for you to talk about these issues. Remember, no one is asking you to talk about sex or anyone's sex life. You're being asked to acknowledge who your employees are and recognize the impact their sexual orientation might have on workplace performance. This book will tell you how to do that.

If you checked group three, congratulations. You've probably done some hard work. To further strengthen your knowledge and skills in this area and get even better teamwork and performance, focus on Chapter 3, *Gaining Skills* and the list of "101 Ways to Make Your Workplace More Inclusive" found in Chapter 5. More than likely, you'll be able to add a number of skills to your already large toolkit.

Whether you placed yourself in group one, two, or three is less important than your willingness to go the next step—to strengthen your knowledge and skills. It's progress—not perfection—that's important. And, most employees, gay and straight alike, will notice and appreciate your efforts to make the workforce all-inclusive. They will also notice if you discriminate or if you stand by doing nothing when discrimination occurs. When this happens, those who consider themselves different from you will be left wondering if they will be the next ones to be discriminated against or excluded.

The fact that you may not already possess a high level of knowledge and skills in this area is nothing to be embarrassed about or ashamed of. Most of us were raised in a heterosexist (placing value only on that which is heterosexual) and homophobic world, so it is not surprising that most people are heterosexist and homophobic. This includes gays, lesbians, bisexuals, and transgender persons as well. The difference is that sexual minorities have often explored and begun to heal their own homophobia.

While we do believe that everyone possesses some homophobia, we don't believe that most managers are blatantly homophobic. Most want to manage all of their employees fairly. However, many simply lack the knowledge, skills, and resources to do that. And, like most people, they tend to ignore issues and situations where they lack these capabilities, as demonstrated in the following two experiences of Bob Powers.

> For years, I have consulted with a small group at one of America's largest firms. It is a group that celebrates weddings, birthdays, anniversaries, engagements and other similar events. It operates in a very collegial fashion. I do not believe there are many people in this group with a blatantly homophobic bone in their body. Yet, six months ago, the group hired a new staff member. He is a 30-year-old man who has a rainbow flag (generally a sign that one is gay—see section on *Getting Familiar with New Communities*) on his computer. He has been in a loving relationship for four years. Yet in this highly social organization, not one person has asked him about his personal life, inquired whether he might be in a relationship, or even remotely broached the subject of his sexual orientation. Neither he nor I believe this stems from homophobia as much as it does from simply not knowing how to talk about these things in a way that does not embarrass him or the person asking. I also believe that if someone were to ask, "What is it like to be a gay man in this group?" or "Are you in a relationship?" or any of hundreds of other questions that would open up discussion in this area, he would be delighted to respond and their

working relationship would be strengthened.

But people are afraid, and not just about gay issues. The fear is about differences. I recently attended a professional conference of an organization dedicated to improving work performance. At the opening event, I spotted, among two thousand participants, a very striking woman. Probably in her mid-forties, she was dressed professionally, *and* she had bright purple hair. I immediately walked over to her and said, "You have purple hair, what's it like?" She beamed and proceeded to tell me how much she enjoyed it. She also said most people in the business world acted as if she didn't have purple hair. We both laughed at the extent of people's denial. I discovered that she was a highly successful management consultant from London, England.

The next day, I addressed a group of 150 or so people and I asked, "How many of you saw the woman with purple hair at the reception last night?" Every hand went up. I then asked, "How many of you were curious about her?" Again, every hand went up. I then asked, "How many of you talked to her?"

Not a single hand was raised.

When asked why, they all basically said the same thing—they were afraid they might embarrass her or themselves, so they did nothing.

The fear of saying or doing the wrong thing is so strong that it often stifles action. As a result, we miss the opportunity to get to know people who are different from us and who can teach us new ways of looking at life, we reinforce hiding, and we lose the chance to improve productivity. Until issues of sexual orientation and other differences are openly addressed and people no longer hide, deny, act up, or stay paralyzed, work productivity and relationships will suffer. If you are still wondering about the relevance of sexual orientation in the workplace, ask yourself this question:

Do I expect that in the next ten or more years gays, lesbians, and bisexuals will be a more or less visible part of the world's workplace?

In answering this question take into account likely political events, recent court actions, scientific discoveries and other relevant trends. If you believe sexual minorities will be a more visible part, then ask yourself:

"Do I want my organization to be known for helping to make the workplace become more inclusive or for working to keep groups of people excluded?"

Sexual orientation, like other forms of diversity, is a relevant workplace issue. When you learn to create a welcoming and inclusive environment for the 25 million gay and lesbian employees and customers, you can expect your employees to go out of their way to ensure that goals and objectives are met and you can expect your customers to go an extra step to buy your products and services.

HOW THIS GUIDE WORKS

A Manager's Guide to Sexual Orientation in the Workplace is laid out to provide you with the knowledge, skills, and resources to attain top-level performance from *all* of your employees.

So far in Chapter 1, you have become familiar with issues in this area and the link between sexual orientation and workplace performance. And, you have probably learned a little about yourself as a manager. You will soon become familiar with the lesbian, gay, and bisexual community and be exposed to the first of many life stories. While unusual in a business book, the life stories serve an important function. They provide you with the knowledge you need to manage effectively. So, you will find, scattered throughout the book, the stories of gays, lesbians, bisexuals, and heterosexuals and how they came to terms with these issues. The first two are those of the authors.

The life stories also form the essence of Chapter 2. In this chapter, you will read about Joe Wilcox, a gay man, and his evening with the company president and his wife. You'll find out why Lisa Busjahn was fired from her company and you'll read the courageous story of one Southern town's "sissy," Rico Hewitt-Cruz. Finally, you'll find out how Jillaine Smith handles her bisexuality.

The stories will prepare you for Chapter 3 where you will begin to build your skills to make the workplace more welcoming and inclusive—more productive, in fact. Based on the premise that people will perform at optimal levels if they have well-defined jobs, know what is expected of them, have the tools, skills, and training to do the job and receive feedback, recognition, and rewards for performing successfully, this chapter introduces you to a performance system, an effective means of attaining high-level performance from all of your employees.

In Chapter 4, you'll read about three heterosexual managers and how they came to terms with these issues. You will discover the impact "Homer the Homo Man" had on Vince Patton when he was growing up in the "Black Bottom" section of Detroit. You'll learn how midwestern values shaped Dale Barr's role as a manager and you will discover how Constance Holmes, who grew up in one of the few all-Black cities in Amercia, deals with these issues.

In Chapter 5, *Making It Work*, you'll learn "101 Ways to Make Your Workplace More Inclusive," a tool to help you put your new-found skills into immediate practice.

In Chapter 6, you will deepen your knowledge of these issues by reading about the family and friends of sexual minorities. Art Moreno, Mick Miller and Luann Conaty will open your heart with their moving tales of how they came to accept the sexual orientation of loved ones, and Frank Wong will open your eyes to the impact culture and society can have on the life of a gay person.

These heartfelt stories will prepare you for the final chapter, *Finding Resources: The Workplace and Beyond*. In Chapter 7, you will discover an abundant list of resources to fill your managerial toolkit. You'll learn about the many organizations in the business world that exist to help you effectively address these issues and how to contact them. You'll be exposed to every major book, news and journal article ever published on the issue of sexual orientation and the workplace, as well as a list of other readings that will help you deepen your knowledge and strengthen your skills.

In all of the above, especially in reading the moving biographies, you'll be asked to open your hearts and your minds. If you do, we guarantee you that the time you spend with this guide will have a very high payoff. You will develop skills that have implications far beyond managing these issues and that is important because the make up of the workplace and the workplace itself are changing rapidly (by the year 2000 white males will be the minority at work). The changes ahead will be of such magnitude and will occur at such a rapid pace that managers who don't keep up will find themselves floundering.

In ever-increasing numbers, sexual minorities are coming out at work. As managers, you need to take advantage of this opportunity to make the workplace more productive and stay afloat in this sea of change. Your responsibility is to welcome and effectively manage *all* people regardless of their color, physical abilities, religion, age, gender, *or* sexual orientation. We think this book will enable you to do exactly that.

Let's begin by getting familiar with the sexual minority community.

GETTING FAMILIAR WITH NEW COMMUNITIES

Many gays and lesbians will tell you that they possess "gaydar," an intuitive ability to spot other gays and lesbians. Few heterosexuals claim this ability. So, how do you know if someone is gay? Frankly, you can't know unless they tell you or provide a clear signal. The lesbian, gay, and bisexual communities signal you in many ways.

Many gays, lesbians, and bisexuals make it easy for you. They speak openly of their sexual identity and generally are quite willing to help you know more about them and the community. Others will do anything to cover up their sexual orientation and it is almost impossible to get to know this group. A third group will talk about their sexual orientation only if asked. If not asked, they generally remain mute (which requires considerable conscious effort and energy). However, this group often displays signs or sends signals that are intended to open the door to those who will ask. Understanding these signs and signals requires you to know more about the community.

To begin, the symbol of gay pride is the rainbow flag. This red, orange, yellow, green, blue, and lavender striped flag symbolizes the diversity in the gay community. It flies from rooftops and is displayed on bumper stickers, lapel pins, and often in the office. (The next time you take a road trip, look for rainbow flags on car bumpers—you'll be surprised by how many you see).

When you see a rainbow flag you can safely assume that whoever is displaying the flag is gay or lesbian or a friend or relative of a gay person. Acknowledging that you recognize the flag is an excellent way to start conversation.

Another symbol is the pink triangle. The triangle represents the patch that gay men were forced to wear in Nazi concentration camps during World War II (lesbians were forced to wear a black triangle). This symbol has deep meaning to gays and lesbians around the world because it depicts the extreme oppression sexual minorities have faced. This symbol is worn today not only as a reminder of that oppression but as a statement that all oppression and hatred must end.

There are many other symbols. At AT&T, many employees (gay and straight alike) post "Safe Place" stickers in a visible spot in their office. These stickers display the pink triangle in a green circle and communicate that this is a safe place to talk. The new DO ASK, DO TELL stickers, available from most bookstores, in effect say the same thing. Ask your openly gay and lesbian employees about these and other symbols. It's another excellent way to open up dialog in this area.

The gay and lesbian community sponsors a number of celebrations and rituals. For example, most sexual minorities celebrate "Gay Pride Day" usually held in the latter half of June. The week-long celebration culminates in "Gay Pride" parades and marches around the world in places such as Sydney, Australia, to Boise, Idaho. For sexual minorities, it is a time to celebrate, not just their sexual orientation, but their courage at coming out despite the oppression they have experienced. These marches draw thousands of people in small towns across the continent and hundreds of thousands in major cities throughout the world. "Gay Pride" day honors the Stonewall riots which occurred in New York City in 1969. On June 25 of that year, sexual minorities (mostly drag queens and lesbians) fought off a police raid of a local bar in Greenwich Village. This rebellion brought people of all sexual orientations together. In honor of the 25th anniversary of Stonewall, over one million people marched down New York's Fifth Avenue in June of 1994. Also celebrated at the same time were the Gay Games—an event of Olympian size proportion (the event at which Greg Louganis "came out" as a gay man). Over 22,000 athletes from around the world participated in these games.

There are hundreds of events like Australia's gay Mardi Gras which attract hundreds of thousands of people annually. These events create sizable business opportunies, as well as a wonderful celebration of freedom and liberation.

Gays and lesbians stay well connected to these and other events through media and social networks. There are hundreds of gay newspapers around the world, and thousands of social, cultural, political, and support groups like gay and lesbian choruses, gay returned peace corps volunteers, gay teachers, and gay police associations. These groups exist in our largest cities and smallest towns. In areas where sexual minorities worry about their safety, these groups often do not use the words gay or lesbian in their titles substituting instead terms related to the community such as pride, triangle, lambda, and so forth.

Additionally, there are hundreds of religious and spiritual groups which attend to the spiritual needs of sexual minorites such as Dignity (Catholic) and Affirmation (Mormons). There are also local and regional business groups like Breakout—a group of lesbian and gay business consultants in San Francisco, the Lesbian and Gay Network of the American Society of Training and Development (ASTD), as well as dozens of organizations that can help you do business in the gay community like the St. Louis Business Guild (see Chapter 7 for a complete listing of these organizations).

DO ASK! DO TELL!

Despite the size of these events and the quantity of these organizations, many people don't even know they exist. The media seldom covers them and, thus, much of what goes on in the community remains closeted. Ironically, the tragedy of AIDS and the publicity of the military's Don't Ask, Don't Tell policies have brought the gay community out of the closet. Tragedy and travesty have a way of bringing people together and causing them to speak out. More than anytime in history, sexual minorities are telling and heterosexuals are asking. This new DO ASK, DO TELL phenomenon will help you to become better educated and to develop the skills that will allow you to effectively manage sexual orientation issues and do business with this sizable community.

Now that you know a little about the community of sexual minorities, let us tell you about us, the authors of this guide.

My Story:

Bob Powers

Management Consultant

When I was little, I knew there was something different about me, but I didn't know what it was. Later, I discovered I was attracted to other boys, and that scared the hell out of me.

I was born in Hastings, Minnesota, in 1941, and soon experienced my fifteen minutes of fame when I was selected the most beautiful baby in Minneapolis, Minnesota. My father also enjoyed some small fame, as he was one of a handful of professional bowlers during that time. Consequently, we were frequently on the move. My mother tells me that she forced my dad to promise that we would settle down when I was big enough that I no longer fit into a hotel dresser drawer. When I was four, we settled in Stockton, California, where I was raised.

My father spent the rest of his career as a life insurance agent. He was moderately successful, and was well-known and well-liked in the community. He was also an alcoholic and gambling addict. These addictions were kept hidden from the children, as was "bad" news and all feelings, except "happy" ones.

My mother was a housewife and she was good at it. She took pride in having a neat and tidy home, as well as neat and tidy kids (I was probably the only kid in school with white polished tennis shoes). My mom had made a "death bed" promise to her father never to touch liquor and this was a promise she kept. She was a strong-willed and independent woman. Growing up, I liked my mom a lot more than I liked my Dad, who was seldom home. I tolerated my two sisters, who were seven and nine years younger than I was. Despite my childish judgments about members of my family, I am still described by my mother as having been an absolutely perfect child.

We were a typical American family, middle-class and very nice. We were also Catholic. My parents never used the word sex in all my growing up. As a result, my discoveries about my sexuality were racked with shame. I don't recall exactly when I realized I was different from other boys. I was probably eleven or twelve when I went to the library to look up the word "homosexuality." I'll never forget what I read. It said "homosexuality: a perversion, a mental illness." I stood there and cried. I didn't feel perverted and I didn't think I was mentally ill. I did not know what to do, so I prayed to God to let me die.

I immediately stopped all activities that I thought were remotely feminine. This led to my denying myself a number of childhood passions. For example, I recall this wonderful old neighbor lady, Mrs. Noyer, who had a big garden, which I just loved. Every day, during the county fair, she would pack up all the neighborhood kids into her car and trek us to the fairgrounds where we would enter flower arrangements. Over the years, I won hundreds of ribbons in the "men's division." I was often written about or pictured, with my arrangements, in the Women's Section of the local newspaper. It was a big thrill for me. I loved this old lady and her garden. But when I came to realize that flowers were "for girls," I abandoned these activities. My fear of being called a pansy was far greater than my passion for growing them. Thirty-five years passed before this passion was rekindled. I was in New Jersey and bent over to smell a geranium. A volcano of feelings erupted and I was overwhelmed with reminiscences of my childhood, the county fair, beautiful flowers, and Mrs. Noyer. I realized there was no longer anything to stop me from gardening. I was queer and everyone who knew me knew I was queer. I spent much of the next several years helping transform an overgrown island into seven acres of paradise.

Growing up, I had two models of a homosexual. One was of a limp-wristed "flaming faggot." I used to practice shaking hands (with myself) in an effort to develop a "manly grip," so that no one would suspect me of being a queer. I spent hours standing in front of a mirror practicing. It never occurred to me that the mirror couldn't help strengthen my grip. The other model, which I created in my imagination, was of a dirty old man in a trench coat. The first time I went into a gay bar, I actually thought I would walk into a room full of men in trench coats. Boy, was I surprised.

I did have some sexual experiences with boys when I was young. Not many. I felt hatred towards them after and lots of shame. I was popular in school and active in student government—I was a real "rah-rah" type. In college I lived for fraternities and parties, and I lived in fear that someone would find out I was really queer. I often went out with girls and prayed I would be attracted to them. And I was attracted to them, but emotionally, rather than physically. I was also selected by a national sorority as one of their "dream men." I was so moved by that gesture, which I thought affirmed my manhood, that I burst into tears in front of ninety young women. Even though I wasn't physically attracted to girls, I could usually be found with a girlfriend. Looking back, I imagine that was one of the ways I protected myself. Another was to gain so much weight that most people simply wouldn't find me attractive.

After graduate school, I went into the Peace Corps. To this day, I don't know where I got the courage to apply. This was a period of time in our country when there was great excitement, generated in large part by the Kennedys. The Peace Corps was newly established and a perfect place for an idealistic young kid like me. But to get in, volunteers went through a lengthy process of extensive FBI screens, numerous psychological tests, and periodic psychiatric and peer evaluations. For months I lived in terror that I'd be found out and that my life would be ruined. Somehow I managed to pass all the cuts. I concluded that I must have fooled everybody, even the experts. The next thing I knew, I was living in a remote village helping develop local business in Malawi, Africa. My Peace Corps experience was transforming. I lived a very simple, yet wonderfully satisfying existence. I rid myself of the weight I had gained and some of the superficial values (the importance of status, possessions, and so forth) I had adopted. I also began to value differences in people. Although I noticed that most Malawians didn't possess the same sexual taboos about homosexuality as Americans— few Malawians would have considered themselves homosexual, yet they freely participated in homosexuals acts—I did not move any closer to accepting my own sexual orientation.

Shortly after joining the Peace Corps, I met a woman and became engaged. As soon as I became engaged, I wanted to be unengaged. I didn't have the courage to be honest about it, so I went about convincing my fiancée that she didn't want to be married to me. I had a couple of other relationships with women and as soon as they got serious, I ran away.

After my two-year Peace Corps stint was up, I travelled through the Middle East and across Europe before returning to the states where, for six months, I taught junior high school. I went back to Malawi on a dual Malawi Government and United States Agency for International Development (USAID) contract, where I worked as a Planning Officer in the Ministry of Natural Resources. I continued to suppress my sexual identity.

In 1969, I returned to the states and went to work for Pacific Telephone, which at the time was a wholly owned subsidiary of AT&T, in San Jose, California. I was in their accelerated management program. I almost wasn't hired because I didn't fit the "management mold"; fortunately, my best friend had enough influence to get me hired anyway. Along with eighteen other overachievers (all of us stated in orientation that we hoped to become CEO), I began a year-long program where I would gradually take on more and more responsibility. At the end of the program, I would either be promoted to middle management or let go. After about nine months, I was told that I had successfully completed the program. I moved into my new assignment where I was responsible for managing sixty or so employees, all women, who handled customer service, order taking, billing, and payments. Although I received little training, I had a knack for managing people. After a couple of years, I was given a job training other managers. I loved it and knew I had found my career niche. Three months later, I was promoted to head the company's management training effort and eventually moved to lead the company's internal management consulting group. These years represented tremendous and rapid professional and personal growth, except in sexual areas.

Early on in my career, I met a woman who constantly made me laugh, and I asked her to marry me. To my surprise, I didn't want to run away and I thought maybe I wasn't queer. I concluded that the only way to know was to get married. I was twenty-eight years old. I remember standing at the altar and saying "I do" and then skipping down the aisle and clicking my heels in the air because I was happy to be married. I thought that meant I wasn't a faggot.

I lived a fairly happy married life. I didn't fool around. We had a beautiful daughter. After about five years of marriage, I went back to New York on business and met an AT&T executive named Robert, a man who came to have a tremendous influence on my life. It turned out that his roommate had served with me in the Peace Corps. Robert invited me to their house for dinner and I enthusiastically accepted. I took the subway to Brooklyn Heights and rang their doorbell. I hardly knew either of these men, yet when they answered the door, I looked at them and burst into tears. I knew they were gay. They were my new role models. They weren't limp-wristed faggots or old men in overcoats. They were simply two nice-looking human beings. At that moment, I also knew beyond a shadow of a doubt I was gay.

I felt as if my life were over. Robert helped me sort through the pain and upheaval that was to come. A short while later, I told my wife I was gay. She was devastated. We stayed together for four more years. During this time, we relocated to New Jersey. We tried hard to make our marriage work, but it didn't work, and we ended it, which was a godsend for both of us. Today, she is happily married and a champion of gay rights. We enjoy a warm and friendly relationship. Courtney, my daughter, was four when I left. Leaving her was the hardest thing I have ever done, for at the time I thought I was a better parent than my wife.

I met Alan fourteen years ago in a Manhattan bar called Boots and Saddles, affectionately known in the gay community as "Bras and Girdles." Alan lived in Chelsea, just outside New York's famed Greenwich Village. I vividly recall our first date. I stood on the street underneath his fourth story window, flowers in one hand and a bottle of Jack Daniels in the other, waiting for him to throw me his key. I felt like a teenager, ready to fall in love. I did.

My daughter came to visit us on our first Christmas together. By then, I had gone through the (terrifying) process of telling my friends and family that I was gay. They were generally supportive. I told them that I was going to tell Courtney, who was still four. Nobody except Alan wanted me to tell her. "Wait until she grows up," they advised. I couldn't, for I knew that if I waited her head would become filled with hated notions about what it meant to be a homosexual, and we might never find a way to communicate.

I said to her, "Courtney, you know how people love one another."

And she said, "Yes."

"Well, some men love other men, like I love Alan." Then I added, "Men who love other men are called homosexuals."

She asked, "What are women who love other women called?"

And I said, "They're called lesbians."

It seemed like an eternity passed as I waited for this four-year-old child to make some sort of pronouncement. She looked at me and said, "Daddy, why do they have such big words?"

Strangely, I knew she understood. She didn't understand the sexual part, but it wasn't about sex, it was about love, and she understood love. I also told her that some people didn't like gay people, that some people might tease her if she decided to tell them and that she had to make a choice to tell them or not. Courtney lived with Alan and me every summer for the next fourteen years. That communication was one of the highlights of my life with my daughter. It gave both of us the opportunity to talk about being gay, and we did, every summer.

I would ask, "Who do you tell?" She would say she tells her friends and I would ask, "What do they say?"

And she would say, "Nothing."

"Nothing"—the word rings in my ears—for it means no hatred, no prejudice, no thing. Today she is a wonderful young woman, unbiased and quite happily heterosexual.

My parents, I learned, wrestled with having a gay son. After a few years together, Alan and I treated them to a two-week visit from California to our home in New Jersey. We set out to give them the time of their lives. The night they left, my father said that while my being gay was initially difficult for them to accept, he wanted us to know that he thought we were the most wonderful couple he had ever known. A short while later, we received a letter from my mother that said their visit was the best two weeks of her entire life. That experience helped me go on to the next step, which was to come out at work.

It was shortly after I met Robert that I moved to New Jersey, the result of a promotion to AT&T headquarters. I became in charge of corporate training. Robert introduced me to the gay underground within the corporation. This was a network of lesbians and gay men, who communicated with one another about corporate policies, people, and events in an effort to survive a homophobic environment. I was amazed that such a group existed and awed by the ease with which it operated and the warm way I was welcomed. This network let me know which managers were particularly homophobic and which were sympathetic, it warned me of impending policies that might impact my future and provided a network of people that I could talk to freely, without fear. It wasn't an organized group, but it was a supportive one.

The final motivation to come out at work came as a result of attending "The Advocate Experience," a weekend workshop which focused on being gay. That experience, along with the realization that the fear of coming out was usually worse than the actual process of coming out, gave me the courage to take this terrifying step. Added to this were the more personal reasons of my desire to stop hiding and telling lies at work and Alan's encouragement to be true to myself. And it was terrifying. I was so scared that I would be fired that each day during this time period I tape recorded who I told, what I said, and how they responded. Thirteen years later, I listened to these tapes and was stunned by the frightened voice I heard. I was also surprised by how thoughtful, organized, and systematic I was in my approach. I had decided not to make a big deal out of it. I made no public announcements. Instead, I told people, one by one, as an occasion presented itself, which was usually a one-on-one meeting. I described the training in which I had participated, the extent to which I hid my sexuality from the person I was telling, and the effect that had on me. For example, I described meeting Alan, falling in love, and how horrible it felt to keep one of the most joyful events in my life a secret because I was afraid. I described how much energy it took to answer everyday questions like "What did you do over the weekend?" or "Are you dating anyone?" and how much conscious thought it took to constantly change the pronoun "he" to "she" so no one would suspect I was a queer. I also told how these little lies reinforced my feeling of shame. But most importantly, I said, the result was I created a distance between us that, for me, was simply unnatural.

Over a period of several weeks, I had told forty or fifty people, who probably told many, many more, that I was gay. It was a remarkable experience. One person after another responded positively. I was deeply moved. The number of insensitive comments made were small in quantity and tone. For example, my boss admonished me for using the word "lover" and, even though she had responsibility for overseeing the corporation's affirmative action/equal opportunity policies, she failed to tell me that I was protected under a corporate antidiscrimination clause that in 1974 was amended to include sexual orientation. Eighteen years passed before I found out that the protection existed back then. A couple of people told me they had heard, second- or third-hand, that a particular person didn't think I needed to make my homosexuality public. Shortly after I came out, my cash vouchers were audited by the company's internal audit staff and the questions they asked and the treatment I received were impertinent, but I have no idea if it had anything to do with my homosexuality. When I asked my boss about it, she said she had no idea and I believed her. Only one event occurred that I'd truly classify as negative. A few weeks after my coming out, I received a phone call from woman who said I had just ruined my career. She was a lesbian, who I believe was frightened by my coming out successfully.

I stayed at AT&T another four years. I consistently received outstanding performance appraisals, was generally ranked at or near the top of middle management performers, received healthy, often substantial, pay raises and was made ready for promotion to the next higher level of management.

I joined a professional society in the early 70s. The National Society for Performance and Instruction (NSPI) is a ten-thousand-person international organization dedicated to improving human performance. About the same time I came out at work, I became very active in NSPI. In some ways, coming out to my professional colleagues was easier than coming out at AT&T, as I often attended NSPI's annual conference with Alan and on many occasions hosted committee and board meetings at our home in New Jersey. In 1981, I was elected vice president of the organization. Three years later, I was elected president of NSPI. In 1992, as cochair of the NSPI's Diversity Committee, I was successful in guiding the executive board to adopt a very inclusive diversity policy, one that reaches out to all people, including gays and lesbians, and stands up against any and all forms of bigotry.

To my knowledge, I have not experienced any form of discrimination based upon sexual orientation within NSPI. I have on a few instances dealt with problems created by homophobia, none of which seemed personally directed at me. Once, when advised that two presenters at the national conference were making homophobic comments, I told them privately that there were people who were offended by such comments and asked them to refrain from making them. They did. NSPI has a large and active military chapter, some of whose members have expressed disagreement with my views around sexual orientation and its relevance in the workplace. But I believe that as a result of my being open and visible, the gap which existed around these points of view has narrowed substantially and many military members have demonstrated, albeit privately, their support and acceptance of me and my stand on these issues. NSPI has been an organization where I have been clearly visible and accepted as a gay man. As a result, I have made substantial contributions to NSPI and, I hope, the profession.

After fourteen years in the Bell System, I left AT&T in 1982 and established my own consulting firm. I had been out in the workplace for four years; I wasn't about to go back into the corporate closet. Yet, in many ways, going out on my own was scarier than coming out at AT&T. Not only was I giving up my financial security, but I was also losing the sense of protection I felt I had in a large corporation. Again, AT&T was remarkably supportive. They gave me my first contract.

I will never forget the day I had my first meeting with a potential client. I was getting dressed when I became overwhelmed with a sense of panic. I thought I had made a huge mistake. In my mind I heard the voice of my self-doubt say, "Nobody wants a fag consultant. Who do you think you are, anyway? You're just ruining your life." Alan came into the dressing room and found me lying on the floor in a fetal position. I managed, through my tears, to tell him I had made a big mistake. Very softly, he said he knew that I would be great and he'd bet that I'd come home afterwards celebrating my first new client. He was right. It was the beginning of a booming, celebrating business. Four years later, I was making a million dollars, working with some of the world's finest corporations as an openly gay consultant.

During this time period, there were many occasions where I was confronted with the choice to tell the truth, and seemingly risk my business, or lie. One of the earliest occasions occurred when I was working with the vice president and treasurer of a large telecommunications company and his five directors, all of whom were straight, white males. I was facilitating a two-day, off-site meeting, and we were discussing staff development. One of the directors turned to me and said, "We were talking at lunch and realized that all of us have the same problem. With all the hours we put into work these days, we hardly see our families anymore and our wives are complaining about it. How do you handle that with your wife?" My mind went nuts! Thoughts of my business folding surfaced like a tidal wave. I felt nauseous and wanted to throw up. Instead, I took a slow, deep breath, looked into the eyes of each of them and said, "My situation is somewhat different from yours in that I live with another man, but let me tell you how I handle the same problem." And I proceeded to tell them. As I spoke I noticed that, one by one, each of them slowly looked in the direction of the vice president (for a signal, I presume) and then back at me. The vice president kept his eyes on me the entire time. I knew he was okay with my sexual orientation, because not only had we discussed it on numerous occasions, but he, his wife, Alan, and I had socialized many times together and enjoyed a longstanding friendship. When I finished speaking there was a slight pause and then one of the directors thanked me, and the conversation resumed as if nothing out of the ordinary had occurred. But it was clear that something extraordinary had just taken place and all seven of us had our way of thinking altered as a result of that exchange. Over time, each of those five directors hired me to work with them and their organizations.

A few years later, I knew I was going to be doing quite a bit of business in Europe. I was advised by a well-meaning colleague that I might want to keep quiet about my sexual orientation. "The Europeans just aren't as accepting as the Americans when it comes to homosexuals," I was told. I was conducting a three-day business-planning session with a group of about twenty middle- to high-level managers from the transportation industry. We were working at a rather luxurious hotel on the coast of Portugal. I had made plans for Alan to join me at the end of the session for a short vacation in Spain. He arrived midway through our work. As I greeted him, several of the participants happened upon us. I felt the same sense of panic I described earlier. I quickly introduced everyone and even more quickly escorted Alan to our room. I felt extremely embarrassed, more that I had succumbed to my colleague's advice, than by the participants' discovery that my partner was a man. At lunch time, several members of the group came to me and insisted that Alan join us for dinner and the evening's planned social activities. He did and, at everyone's insistence, he was back the following day. I was taken aback by how natural it was. I went on to do much additional work with this group and was referred by them to others within their corporation.

Another occasion occurred when *Training* magazine wanted to do a profile on me. During the interview, I spoke of being gay and the relevance I thought it had to my work. To speak out about being a gay man gave me the illusion that I had control over who knew. But for some reason, the idea of seeing my name in print as a gay man gave me no sense of control over who knew. That frightened me. The subject matter frightened the editorial board at *Training* magazine, who had never before printed the word "gay." It was one of the first professional publications to recognize the relevance being gay has to the workplace. The profile entitled, "Bob Powers: An Unconventional Success Story," was published in August 1986. It did shock me when I saw my name written in conjunction with being gay, but I got over it and soon saw myself written up as a gay man in numerous publications.

By the mid-1980s my business was booming. I employed several people and co-owned a second consulting firm with offices in California and England. On any given day, I could be found in first class on TWA, British Airways, or the Concorde, flying between New York, London, and San Francisco. Or, if I wasn't on an airplane, I might be huddled with a group of high-level executives or advising a cadre of newly hired Harvard and Stanford MBAs. I was becoming, I thought, a terribly important consultant and very impressive person.

I began to add to the property I already owned, namely, a rental unit in California and our home, an eight-bedroom, converted grist mill on a seven-acre island in Three Bridges, New Jersey. I purchased a chic Manhattan loft overlooking the Empire State Building, a four-bedroom San Francisco co-op overlooking the Golden Gate Bridge, and a small "villa" a few steps off the Mediterranean in Marbella, Spain. My life looked like a fairy tale. In reality, it was becoming a nightmare.

I let the glamour and excitement of my new success almost ruin my life. I was constantly away from home. While I had friends all over the world, I didn't have a single friend at home. I lost whatever humility I had and replaced it with self-importance. I also added weight. I became fat, mentally and physically. I was also destroying my relationship with the one person in the world I most loved, Alan.

In 1989, I began to make major changes in an effort to simplify my life. I reduced both my workload and income substantially. I spent most of my time at home. I wrote and completed two books. I acted in community theater. And, as I mentioned, I played in my garden. I also began to do some hard physical, therapeutic, and spiritual work, as well. That same year I became active in a twelve-step program for people affected by another's alcoholism. I joined a gym and lost the weight I gained, and I sought therapy. In addition, I became active in what has to be America's most diverse and accepting spiritual community, Glide Memorial Methodist Church in San Francisco, where I now live. All of the above have helped me through a difficult set of years. After fourteen years together, Alan and I ended our relationship in 1992. I don't know how I would have survived the pain I experienced as a result of parting without having undergone the changes that have occurred in me over these past four years.

Today, I live like a regular human being. The experiences of my past seem to make sense today.

Given the extent to which I used to hide my being gay, and given how openly I live my life today, I find great irony in the following tale, especially for what it says about who we fool when we hide. It was Halloween day, 1971. And I thought I was straight.

In keeping with the custom of the phone company, I decided to dress in costume. As if I hadn't a fear in the world, I donned a wig, a two-piece woman's suit, high heels, handbag, and pill box hat. I added makeup, nail polish, and a few accessories. I was completely in drag. Since I wanted to surprise the sixty or so women who worked in the office, I sneaked through the building's back door and began to hobble my way down the long, sterile corridor. About midway to my desk, I started to feel dizzy and within seconds I passed out. Now, here I was, a total closet case, looking like a poor imitation of Bette Davis, spread-eagle on the cold, hard tile of Pacific Telephone's Santa Clara Business Office. I came to and looked up into the blurry but smiling faces of the twenty-five or thirty women hovering above me. *And, I thought I wasn't queer.*

My Story:

Alan Ellis

University Professor

I was born in the shadows of the Wasatch range of the Rocky Mountains at Latter-Day Saint Hospital in Salt Lake City, Utah. The date was November 23, 1957.

I have often thought that being born in Utah in 1957 was like being born in 1937—socially and culturally—anywhere else in the United States. I was raised a Mormon. My family's history in the church dates back to the 1850s and both my father's and mother's grandfathers were polygamists and each had two wives. My father was an accountant and did well in his work. In the latter years of his career, he started a number of small businesses with his younger brother. I felt that his work and desire to provide for our family were more important to him than the church, although he was always active in the ward (the local congregation). My mother's commitment to the church was never in question and she raised us to be equally committed as Mormons. For the first twenty-five years of my life, she was successful—my world view was entirely filtered through a Mormon lens.

My memory of the assassination of John F. Kennedy illustrates the extent to which the church dominated my early existence. I was told that the President was shot one day before my sixth birthday. I was aware of only one president—the one who headed three million Mormons. Imagine my surprise, four months later when the president of the church spoke at our April conference. I assumed he had been resurrected, further evidence of the veracity of the Mormon Church.

At the age of twelve, I began to hear the words "faggot," "homo," and "queer." Initially, I had little idea what they meant but it was clear they were meant to be cruel. I began to wonder if these words had something to do with me.

About this same time, I recall having sexual fantasies that included other boys. Perhaps, in response to these fantasies, I developed a number of strange fears and beliefs. One of these had to do with my body. I was fourteen and my family had flown to Washington, D. C., to visit relatives. It was August: hazy, hot, and humid. My uncle and aunt invited all of us to go to the community pool. I was tall and thin. For some reason, I concluded that my bony hips were too large for a male body and I panicked, thinking they would reveal I was queer. I refused to go swimming.

When we returned home, I walked a little over a mile in pouring rain to a public telephone booth and called a psychiatrist. I pleaded for help. I tried to strike a bargain in which he would help me find girls attractive and I would pay him back when I was old enough to get a job. He seemed a bit surprised by my request and suggested that I contact the county mental health services where I would not have to worry about payment. I did. For several months, I rode my bike ten miles each way and paid two dollars per visit to see a psychologist, who eventually suggested that I was too young to know what my lifelong sexual desires would be and that I shouldn't worry so much about it.

During this time, I heard only veiled reference to homosexuality by the leaders of the church. However, there was much said about the evils of masturbation and, like a good Mormon, I religiously attempted to avoid this "sordid" activity. It was during this period that my mother, after twenty-nine years of marriage, divorced my father. As far back as I can recall, I knew my mother slept downstairs while my father slept upstairs. As they so seldom displayed any tenderness or emotion, the divorce didn't seem to change much—they simply slept in different houses now.

At the age of nineteen, I went on a two-year mission to spread the Mormon teachings to Buenos Aires, Argentina. The experience of living in another country helped me see that there were many ways to live and, at some level, I acknowledged that most, if not all, were equally "correct" ways to conduct one's life. Nevertheless, I remained convinced that the Mormon Church was the true church and I hoped that serving a mission would convince God that I was committed enough to be granted my long-sought after goal to be attracted to women.

Upon my return to the States, I began classes at Brigham Young University. Like my father, I majored in accounting, and I did well. I taught Spanish at the language training center where missionaries were trained and I was the executive secretary to the bishop of my congregation. All of my sexual energy was sublimated into my work, which I loved, especially teaching and counseling missionaries. My involvement in the church was extensive and, in a sense, I was on the "fast-track" within the Mormon hierarchy.

During this period, however, I spent innumerable late nights walking around Provo, Utah, pondering and lamenting my sexual attraction to men. I developed strong feelings toward a number of my male college friends and some of the missionaries I was teaching, but I did not act on them.

I "fell in love" with one of my roommates, an attractive and fully alive man, who had cystic fibrosis. Because of his condition, he needed someone to pound on his chest once or twice a day to clear his lungs. I enjoyed being able to help him in this way and this "acceptable" physical contact increased my attachment to him. We shared a small dorm room with beds that were within reach of each other. The sexual energy between us was strong but we never openly discussed it. There were occasions, in the wee hours of the morning, when he would encourage me to pet his genitals. I recall shaking in my bed as I attempted to avoid giving in to the temptation while deeply longing to have this contact with him. On occasion, the longing won out. He acted as if he were in a dream state, saying his girlfriend's name (we all had "girlfriends" at the time) as I petted him. On the days following this activity, I felt unbelievable guilt. And, although my roommate attempted to talk me out of it, I went to confess to the bishop who, in no uncertain terms, told me that this behavior must never happen again. He placed me on probation (a form of punishment in the church) and arranged for me to see a psychologist employed by the church.

The psychologist believed that homosexuality was a choice that could be cured, and he set out to change me. His method was strange. We took walks during which he encouraged me to look at women and imagine what they were thinking. He believed that homosexuality was simply an inability to understand women. Since I had little sexual contact with either men or women, he considered me an easy prospect for cure. I told him about a dream in which I was physically, though not sexually, intimate with a woman. He took that as sufficient evidence that I had changed and declared me "cured." I was very hopeful that his diagnosis was correct, but the "cure" was fleeting and I soon began to long for my former roommate. I wept as I thought of him and fantasized that we could disappear together to a place where neither my family nor friends would be hurt by our relationship.

In December of 1981, I completed my degree in accounting and left Utah to work as an internal auditor for a company in Minneapolis. On my way, I spent the night in Cheyenne, Wyoming. I went to a bookstore where I noticed that there was a section for pornography. I was shocked to see that some of the magazines had men on the covers. My heart began to pound. Although I was twenty-four, I had no idea that such magazines existed. Despite my embarrassment, I bought two.

They had a strong impact on me because their existence meant that there must be many other men just like me. While I was pleased to recognize that, I simply couldn't imagine what it would be like to live as a gay man. I destroyed the magazines within hours of purchasing them. Again, I prayed that I would awake to find myself sexually attracted to women.

My work involved constant travel across the United States and Latin America. I spent many nights in Holiday Inns wondering what to do about my sexual identity. I seldom thought about my work as an auditor, at which I was quite successful. I had yet to violate any of the significant standards of the Church. I didn't even drink caffeinated soda.

At the end of one year, I quit my job. My managers believed that I quit because I had not been challenged by the work. That thought never even entered my mind. I left because I was simply too absorbed by the conflict between my sexual identity and my religious beliefs to focus on my work as an internal auditor. At the time, I knew of no one to whom I could turn for help either within the company or in the Minneapolis community.

I returned to school in January of 1983 and went on to receive a second bachelor's degree in psychology from the University of Utah. For the most part, I could not think of anything better to do. I took a course in social psychology that led me to question the teachings of the Mormon Church. The structure of my belief system began to crumble and so did the major stumbling blocks to dealing with my sexuality.

Even so, I had not rid myself of society's homophobic messages which I had deeply internalized. In a final desperate act, I borrowed money from my father to engage in a form of therapy that promised a cure. It was called aversion therapy, a nice term for shock treatments. During these sessions, the therapist attached electrodes to my arm and a plethysmograph to my penis. Then, he showed me videos involving sex between two men. Whenever I responded physically to the videos, I would be shocked.

Several months after the therapy ended, I met a woman in one of my psychology classes, and we began to date. I was twenty-five and a virgin. We had sex and I took this as a sign that the therapy had been successful. My relief was short-lived however, and to my dismay, I found myself even more attracted to some of the men I saw the following day. I continued to date and have sex with this woman for two months but it quickly became apparent to both of us that something was wrong. I concluded that I could not successfully explore my sexuality in Salt Lake City.

I went to the library to look at a number of Sunday papers from various cities to check the want ads. As I thumbed through the Seattle paper I came across an article that featured gay Seattle and included a reference to a gay Mormon group. Two days later, I moved to Seattle with four hundred dollars and a carload of belongings. I was so filled with fear that I waited six weeks before contacting the Mormon group. With great difficulty, I met with the contact person. Even though I knew he was gay (and he obviously knew I was), I couldn't, after so many years of fighting it, bring myself to say the words, "I am gay."

Shortly after I arrived, I got a job as an assistant supervisor for billing in the printing department at the University of Washington. The supervisor seemed to like me and I trusted her; even so, I kept quiet about my sexual orientation.

I participated in my first Gay Pride Day that summer. I was thrilled to be among so many other gays and lesbians, whose presence was still a marvel to me. Following the parade, I went to a movie with the contact person of the Mormon group. To my horror, my supervisor sat in the row in front of us. I panicked. I was sure that my male friend's "obvious" gayness would give me away, and my supervisor would know I was a homosexual. I wasn't ready for that so I pretended not to see her. Soon I heard her mention to her friend that someone she knew (me) seemed to be avoiding her. I felt like a fool and clumsily said hello. I was evasive in introducing my friend and I mumbled and stuttered through the conversation. The movie was a blur. I dreaded going into work the next day. To my great relief, my supervisor sensed that I was having difficulty and took me out for a lunch that included a strong drink. I had only recently started drinking and it had quite an effect. She said that my being gay was not an issue for her, that it was fine. I was thankful and relieved and I was struck by the thought that my first experience at coming out to a heterosexual was traumatic primarily because of my own fears.

In August, I moved to Champaign, Illinois, to begin graduate work in psychology at the University of Illinois. I stopped in Salt Lake City to visit my family. Although I had not intended to tell any of them about my sexual orientation, I surprised myself by telling my sister. I knew that my sister and her boyfriend socialized with a gay couple; still, it was very difficult to tell her. She was very supportive. She said she was also surprised. I had succeeded rather well at "acting straight."

When I arrived in Champaign, I reentered the closet that I had so tentatively left in Seattle. I was afraid that my professors would flunk me if my sexual orientation were known. There were no graduate students or faculty visibly "out" in the department, so there was no way to assess how anyone might react to my sexual orientation. I felt weak and cowardly. My first semester was marked by academic success but my discomfort over hiding my sexuality grew. I had a hard time trying to integrate who I was as a person with my role as a graduate student.

I decided to come out to another student who I thought might also be gay. I hemmed and hawed, trying to tell him. He finally asked if I was gay and if I thought he was. I said "yes," and he turned out to be very supportive even though he was straight. We subsequently talked at length about my sexual identity. Whenever I would wonder why I was gay, he would respond matter of factly, "Well, who better than you?" He helped me survive that first semester.

During the second semester, I joined a gay and lesbian support group at a local church, even though I had begun to think of myself as an agnostic. The support group offered an environment in which I felt safe to discuss my fears and, as a result, I was able to come out to several of my fellow students that semester.

Even though I continued to worry about how people would react, I stepped further out of the closet. I became involved with the university's gay and lesbian organization which was holding demonstrations to have sexual orientation added to the nondiscrimination clause. The Chancellor appointed a task force on sexual orientation which I was asked to join. My name was in the student newspaper on several occasions because of my participation. The first time that happened I stayed home out of fear of the reaction that might occur. That evening I called several of my friends to find out how people had reacted and found out there was little reaction and what there was had been supportive.

During this time, I had distanced myself considerably from everyone in my family with the exception of my sister. I could not envision ever telling the rest of my family, especially my parents. It seemed ironic and saddened me that thirty thousand students knew I was gay, but my family didn't. I became determined to tell them. I tried to reassure myself by concluding that their reaction would not greatly alter my daily existence—they could either disown me or get to know me better. Finally, I mustered my courage and when I flew home over spring break, I told them I was gay. My father seemed resigned and somewhat accepting. He said that he had always heard that one in ten were homosexuals and that there was little they could do about it. I was surprised that he knew that much. He went on to say that he had five children (inferring that there was a reasonable probability that one would be gay) but that he hadn't really thought about it.

My mother's response was quite different. In a tone that sounded somewhat like an accusation, she asked, "But you don't live that way do you?" I pretended that I didn't know what she meant by the question and let it go. It had been extremely difficult for me to tell her so I simply left, satisfied that I had told her. I knew it would take time for her to process it as it would take time for me to share more about my life with her.

I continued to serve on the Chancellor's Task Force. My dissertation chairperson asked why I was involved. I told him that it was a good opportunity to use some of my statistical skills and that it was personally important to me since I was gay. He told me that he objected to homosexuality, but said that my sexual orientation would have nothing to do with our professional relationship. Many of my friends suggested that I change dissertation chairs, but I knew that he had recently written a glowing letter of recommendation for a gay student who was going to graduate school. He provided me with a research assistantship from his grant's travel funds that greatly facilitated completion of my dissertation. The Task Force was successful in getting the Chancellor to sign an executive order adding sexual orientation to the university's nondiscrimination clause. The order had little legal power but it was an important symbolic victory.

I was now completely "out" (or so I thought) and was about to complete my Ph.D. I had enjoyed graduate school and was ready to enter the job market. I listed my participation on the Chancellor's Task Force on my curriculum vitae and was advised by my dissertation chair that I should remove it. He suggested that, in a tough job market, the inclusion of the Task Force might reduce or eliminate my chances for a good job. I removed the reference, succumbing once again to well-meaning advice and throwing myself back into the closet.

I was invited to join the faculty at the University of Kentucky (UK) in Lexington. UK is only five hours by car from Champaign. I was involved in a relatively new relationship at the time and the short distance was one of the factors that influenced my decision to accept the position. The psychology department at UK was well-respected and I found the department matched my temperament. I also found a larger gay and lesbian community than in Champaign, even though the community in Lexington was much more underground. Several of my fellow graduate students suggested that I avoid living in Kentucky because of the many fundamentalists in the state. But, the move felt right at the time, so I began a career as a college professor in August 1988.

Because there was no reference to my sexual orientation, I had to come out all over again. I began by telling some of my colleagues and asked them to feel free to tell others, especially if someone asked. Despite this permission, many guarded the information even when asked directly by others. It was clear to me that they, too, had been influenced by society's homophobia and found it difficult to come out for me. To facilitate my coming out, I joined the Association of Gay and Lesbian Psychologists and listed it on my curriculum vitae. In addition, I began to do research on gay and lesbian issues. My colleagues and graduate students were supportive. Although I never came out directly in the classroom, I often spoke of gay and lesbian concerns when we discussed such issues as discrimination and prejudice in the courses that I taught.

I felt somewhat protected by the American Psychological Association's strong support for diversity. Even so, I experienced the effects of homophobia when a lesbian faculty member and I indicated interest in teaching a course on gay and lesbian issues. The Director of Women's Studies implied that if we were to teach such a course we would be unlikely to be granted tenure.

By now, my sexuality was fairly well integrated into my personal and professional life. With the exception of my sister, my relationship with my family centered on ignoring what I had told them several years earlier. Admittedly, much of this was a result of my not disclosing much about my personal life when I visited. However, it was clear that it remained an uncomfortable topic for most of my family. The few times my mother and I did discuss it we tended to do so in a very academic and intellectual way. My mother read books on the subject but they generally were limited to those focusing on how to "cure" homosexuality. She sent me piles of brochures and such from Homosexuals Anonymous and Evangelicals Concerned, so-called religious organizations that claim to have cured homosexuals. I simply threw them in the garbage.

Last year I felt it was time to discuss more fully my sexual orientation with my family, with my mother in particular. I told her that my sexual orientation is not simply some intellectual decision that I had made but that it is who I am. I told her I have been in a number of relationships with other men and that my sexual identity is a part of both my personal and professional identity. Not only am I gay, but I do research on gay and lesbian issues, much of which is published in national and international journals. She seemed accepting, but then surprised me with the news that she had written a brochure that theorized why I was gay. She told me that she was self-publishing the brochure and making it available to Homosexuals Anonymous since she believed that it offered support for a cure.

While I wish my mother would accept me for who I am,

including my gay identity, I realize that on the issue of my sexuality we may never agree. My mother remains very active in the Mormon Church—she is now on a mission for the church in England. She just celebrated her seventieth birthday and it is doubtful that she will ever substantially change her opinions on homosexuality. I do feel that she respects me for my accomplishments and that she loves me. For that, I am grateful. However, I regret that, despite her intentions, her writing is hurtful to me and to other gays and lesbians.

As I look back on my first thirty-five years, I wonder about the impact that being gay has had on my life. No doubt it has influenced how I accept and express who I am. Indeed, who I am today, the sensitivities that I have toward others and their experiences, and the connections that I feel to others who are oppressed, are the direct result of my sexual orientation. At seventeen, I remember staring at a dark and overcast sky and begging God to change my attraction to men. Today, I am grateful for what being gay has taught me.

Gaining Knowledge

2

Learning From Life Stories

The stories you are about to read in this and the following chapters are remarkable protraits of people from various walks of life and corners of the world. They represent people of varying race, age, gender, creed, geographic location, and profession. The stories are divided into three groups. The first group are stories of gay, lesbian, and bisexual employees. The second group are stories of diversity–sensitive heterosexual managers and the final group are stories which focus on family and friends and the impact of society and culture on sexual orientation.

The people whose stories appear here were selected, not because they have disastrous workplace stories to tell, not even because they were particularly discriminated against. They were selected because they were willing to tell the truth about their lives. That meant they had to be "out" about their sexual orientation or if they are heterosexual, they had to speak out about their acceptance of sexual minorities. That was the criteria Rico followed in telling what it was like to begin life as one Southern town's sissy, as well as Luann who writes of her fifty-plus years as a Christian fundamentalist, and Vince, a high-ranking military man who tells about his boyhood encounters with "Homer the Homo Man" and describes how these encounters altered his life forever.

WHAT LIFE STORIES TELL US

As you will read, the decision to be "out" at work poses many conflicts for the majority of sexual minorities. These conflicts also exist for heterosexuals in deciding to tell others about a gay parent, sibling, child, relative, friend, or coworker. You will see these and other conflicts, as well as unheralded and courageous acts vividly depicted as you read through the eleven life stories. You will also read about experiences, such as teen suicide, physical abuse, and alchoholism that may cause you to question why these are being spoken of in stories related to sexual orientation and the workplace. As you will discover, for most people it is impossible to compartmentalize and separate such issues. They affect who we are and what we bring with us into the workplace, and so they too affect our performance.

Some of the issues presented in the stories are difficult, if not painful, to read. We recognize that open discussion of these issues and experiences may make it appear to some readers that the experiences are unique to gay men and women. In reality, many of the difficult and painful experiences described in this book are all too common in society and the difference here is not the occurrence of such experiences in our storytellers' lives but the open discussion of them.

While it is impossible to represent every person in eleven stories, we think that you will discover a part of yourself in these stories, regardless of your sexual orientation. For these are the stories of human beings. These are your coworkers, your employees, your bosses, and your customers. Because of the openness and willingness of our storytellers, you will gain unique and valuable knowledge of the issues that affect the lives of sexual minorities and their families and friends and their relationship to work.

COWORKER, EMPLOYEE, BOSS: GAY, LESBIAN, BISEXUAL

In this chapter, you will be introduced to four members of the gay, lesbian, and bisexual community—Joe Wilcox, Lisa Busjahn, Rico Hewitt-Cruz, and Jillaine Smith—and to their unique experiences. Their stories illustrate both the commonalities and differences that one can experience as a gay or bisexual woman or man. As you read them, you will notice that most of these storytellers, like the authors, began their journey denying their sexual orientation or feeling great shame as they recognized in themselves something that they were told was perverted, evil, and wrong. This discrepancy between what they were gradually realizing about who they were and the (negative) messages associated with that identity was terrifying. And, in several cases, religion and other societal institutions played strong roles in that terror (as in Alan's experience within the Mormon church and Bob's experience at the library). In all of these stories, however, you will witness a journey from that place of shame and denial to a place of self-awareness and acceptance.

In Joe Wilcox's story, you'll discover how a simple company dinner can pose a special challenge to sexual minorities. In Lisa Busjahn's story, you'll see how negative attitudes disrupt productive work relationships and divert energy from organizational goals to efforts to protect oneself. Rico Hewitt-Cruz's childhood experiences will tear at your heart. Yet, his story is one of courage in overcoming overt prejudice and finding self-acceptance in the military and later in life. In Jillaine Smith's story, you will experience the unique challenges that bisexuals face in society and the work world and begin to understand the importance of inclusion of *all* sexual minorities.

Joe Wilcox   Human Resources Professional

I was raised in a large Catholic home in suburban New Jersey with four brothers and two sisters. While I can't say that my childhood was idyllic, I considered it relatively normal as compared with other kids. I recall that my parents weren't demonstrative in their expression of emotions, and throughout my childhood I tried to be perfect in order to garner their affection and approval. This perfectionism showed up in my schoolwork, in the work I did around the house, and even in the way I related to my brothers, sisters, and friends. Being polite and well mannered were always extremely important to me. To this day, these manners can be seen in my work life and relationships.

As I grew older and reached the age

of twelve or thirteen, when many boys started becoming interested in girls, I began to worry much of the time about my ambivalent feelings toward girls. While I always enjoyed being around girls, there were no new feelings inside me that compelled me to want to write notes to girls or carry their books. I began to do those things anyway in order to be like my peers and attributed my disinterest to the thought that I must be very late in maturing and that those feelings would come when I matured.

I had been minimally exposed to homosexuality through stereotypes on television and the comments of my friends. When I began to mature, I was disturbed to notice that my fantasies generally did not include girls, but centered on men or other boys in my life. I looked up the word "faggot" in the dictionary—a bundle of sticks used to start fires. Not much help. Later, I learned that those bundles were used to burn witches, heretics, and homosexuals. I read in another book that many adolescents go through a phase in which they have homosexual feelings. Greatly relieved, I looked forward to passing through and beyond this unpleasant phase of my life.

In the interim, I had two minor affairs with boys toward the end of my high school days. I tried to put this "phase" behind me. In anticipation of becoming a healthy heterosexual, I began to look at women and comment on their physical attributes to some of my friends. I collected the requisite pinups of the time—Linda Ronstadt and Loni Anderson—despite the fact that I still couldn't understand the attraction. I decided that by doing the things my straight friends did I would become more like them and hopefully hide my secret at the same time.

It became more and more difficult to deny the fact that I was gay. But because of my religious beliefs, I continued to suppress my feelings toward other men, and I propagated the lie that I was a heterosexual. I tried even harder to attain a "normal" life by starting a relationship with a female friend of mine. It didn't take long till we were seeing each other seriously, and the prospect of sex became imminent. I found myself in situations in which I'm certain other men would have known what to do and the situations would have resulted in sex. With me, however, they never advanced beyond necking sessions.

Thankfully, after a year of dating, she broke off the relationship to begin seeing a mutual friend. I acted upset, although inside I was relieved that the pressure was off, and I would only have to talk about women and not feel impelled to perform.

In my junior year of college, I was assigned a roommate in the dorm and found myself attracted to him. I began to unravel the lie I had perpetuated of being straight and started to admit to myself that maybe these feelings weren't a phase after all. Coincidentally, I also started to wonder if my roommate might be gay. I listened to some of his phone conversations and watched for any hints in his behavior that would tell me about his sexual orientation. Finally, I read a card from a man I had believed to be his lover. The card confirmed to me that he was gay, and I confronted him with the knowledge. Ironically, it was this discussion that began my coming-out process, wherein I admitted to myself and to my roommate that I was gay. Though we never did have a physical relationship, we often went out together and met many other gay men who went to our college. I will always be grateful to him for introducing me to gay life.

I did a lot of carousing during my last two years of college. I was very conservative in choosing partners, however, and I was determined to find a long-term partner, whereas many of the men I met were only interested in short-term or no-term relationships.

I stayed very secretive about being gay and told no one except other gays. The only exception to this was when I told a woman whom I had recently met at college. She told three of the friends I had established in prior years. "I just don't want to hear about it," one of them said, and all three began to distance themselves from me.

My first job after school was as an insurance and patient billing coordinator in a large clinic. The atmosphere was very open, and I knew many of the people I worked with from outside organizations. I told many of my co-workers that I was gay. They seemed to accept it well. In retrospect, the environment in that office allowed me to be myself and without the constant worry of being discovered, I was able to give most of my energy to my job.

While everyone I worked with knew I was gay, I was still unable to come out to my family. I was simply too afraid. There was an often-told story in my family about one of my brothers who used to go out with his high school friends to pick up gays at a local cruising spot and then beat them up. This story was always good for a laugh. They laughed especially hard at the notion of harming an "unsuspecting, nellie faggot." I would pretend to enjoy the story, but my insides hurt each time I heard them speak. I learned that cruising in public places was dangerous with people the likes of my brothers around.

When my father died while I was still in high school, I actually felt somewhat relieved that I wouldn't have to tell him about my being homosexual. In fact, I was so afraid of the prospect that my family would disapprove that I moved out of the house and decided never to tell them about myself.

At the age of twenty-two, I began a relationship that I call my first real love. Keeping the relationship secret from my family became increasingly stressful. Then, too, I had difficulty reconciling my sexuality with the rules of the Catholic Church. I began consulting and confessing with a priest on a weekly basis to try to come up with some way that I could continue to practice Catholicism and still maintain my relationship. The pressure was intense. The lack of integrity I had with my family, the idea that I might have to leave the church, which had been a source of great comfort to me in the past, and the day-to-day stresses of maintaining a relationship were too much for me. I was overwhelmed with conflict and shame. Shortly thereafter, each of these pressures was resolved.

First, I was involved in a car accident, which required me to live with my family for a short period of time. During that time, my mother read one of my personal journals, which described in detail my relationship with my lover. She wasn't happy, nor did she confront me directly. However, my sister did, and I ended up coming out to her. Before long, I was out to my entire family.

Then, after two years of being together, my lover left me. It was extremely upsetting, yet it propelled me to develop a network of friends that were able to help me get through a difficult time. I took the breakup as an opportunity to make some other big changes in my life.

I did some very deep soul searching where I seriously considered joining the priesthood. I realized that I could never maintain a vow of celibacy. By now, I had developed a very close relationship with God and had a very clear experience of who God was in my life, which was different from what was being taught by the Catholic Church. Soon, I chose to leave the Catholic Church.

During this time, I changed jobs and went to work within the corporate offices of Manufacturer's Hanover Trust, a very conservative New York City bank. I threw myself back into the closet, where I suppressed my enthusiasm, creativity, and energy. I commuted to work by train, from New Jersey to Manhattan, every day and developed a small group of commuter friends, especially two men and two women. One of the men, Donald, lived near me, and we would walk from the station to our neighborhood. Soon, I began to wonder if he might be gay. I dropped a few "hints" and found out my suspicions were accurate. Donald and I became very friendly after that. He sometimes became the topic of discussion with the other commuters. One of the women told me that the others thought that "Donald was a faggot," but she didn't believe it because he had a beard and moustache. This bit of information panicked me and I made sure that I never gave any of them any indication that I too might be a faggot.

Working in New York was exciting (my father had commuted to New York as an executive, and I had always aspired to do the same), but my job wasn't. In an effort to hide my home life, I acted very serious and businesslike. As a result, my employers saw me as dull and lifeless. They treated me as if I weren't able to pick things up quickly, though in fact I learned quickly and was bored by most of what I did. Their assessments of me in performance reviews were always adequate or good, but in their eyes I never excelled. This was an enormous change from the way I was perceived at the doctor's clinic, and it was a difficult one for me to accept, as I felt devalued.

During my first year working in New York I went out a lot. I missed living with someone and I was very lonesome. I wanted to share my life. I had a very good friend with similar aspirations, and together we cruised the only known social outlet for gays—the bars—looking for mates. In 1985, I met Thaddeus. We began to see each other seriously and soon fell in love. After three months we decided to live together.

Even though I still seldom discussed my lifestyle with my family, I wanted them to know Thaddeus and to know that I thought of him as my life partner. Finally, something happened that brought me fully out of the closet with my family. Thaddeus and I were preparing to celebrate our second Christmas together. My mother decided that she wanted all of her children, sons-in-law, daughters-in-law, and grandchildren to come home for Christmas. For the event, she scheduled a well-known photographer to take a family portrait. Since I had made it clear that Thaddeus was my spouse, he was invited with all the other in-laws. It was Christmas Eve day and our house was extremely chaotic. Eighteen of us—my mother, seven children, four in-laws, and six grandchildren—all were crammed into my mother's house for the holiday photo session.

When the photographer arrived, she busied herself with the equipment, as my mother gathered all of her brood into the living room for the photo shoot. The photographer then began to arrange people. She put my two oldest brothers with their wives and children and then she pointed to me and asked, "Are you married?" For the very first time that day, my entire family fell silent. Not even a peep was heard from the babies. I mumbled an affirmative grunt, and she asked, "Where is your lovely wife?" I thought my entire family would die. I pointed to Thaddeus and she looked behind him and asked again where she was. This time, through my embarrassment, I distinctly pointed him out. She looked at us both and put us into position. She then went to my next brother and asked, "Are you married?" When he said, "Yes," she added, "To what?" At that, everyone broke into hysterical laughter. Regaining her composure, the photographer began shooting away.

This incident gave my family what they needed to make my homosexuality okay with them. It also made possible subsequent discussions that since have made it comfortable for me to be gay with my family. And, in some way, it educated the photographer to think twice before automatically assuming everyone is a heterosexual.

By now, I was out everywhere but work. After two years at the bank, I changed jobs and joined Atlantic Mutual, a mid-sized insurance company based on Wall Street, working in the Human Resources department. The company had been established for one hundred and fifty years and was considered one of the more conservative companies in the industry. At first, I opted to keep secret about being gay for fear of losing my job. While I was certain that my bosses wouldn't have fired me solely for being gay, they might have felt it was "poor judgment" to come out and use that as the reason for losing trust in me.

I excelled quickly at my new job as an analyst and began to establish myself as a hard-working and energetic employee. I was quick to take on additional responsibilities and was viewed favorably by most of the people with whom I worked. Soon I was promoted to supervisor and then to manager.

By the time I had been with the company for five years, I had slowly picked out people with whom I worked that I felt I could trust, and I told them the "secret" of my sexuality. Then something happened that made me realize that my secret was not quite as hidden as I had thought. Following a day of heavy snow, my supervisor informed me that she had tried to call me to let me know that the office would be closed. When the operator couldn't find my name listed with directory assistance, my supervisor said that she tried to remember my roommate's name. I was shocked that she knew I had a roommate. As casually as I could, I asked how she knew my roommate's name. She told me that she had seen it on my life insurance beneficiary information.

I used that opportunity to begin talking more freely about Thaddeus. I spoke of vacations we had taken, mentioned our checkbook in conversations, and told about our sharing a car. I even brought Thaddeus to the annual holiday party. I made it apparent to everyone that Thaddeus was more than just a roommate.

About this time, I became more socially and politically aware. I read everything I could about gay and lesbian issues. Soon, I realized that by being open at work I could help represent gays and lesbians as being visible and equal (and sometimes superior) contributors to the work force, which led me to an important decision. I would discuss being gay as if I were straight. For example, if someone asked me about my personal life, I would feel free to tell them about my relationship with Thaddeus, if that was pertinent.

The first few times I said the word gay in public, I could feel my ears turn red and the room get warmer as I waited for a reaction, positive or negative. Sometimes the words rang very hollowly in my head as I confronted the awkward situations these conversations seemed to create. But mostly, I felt freedom and that outweighed the slight embarrassment I sometimes felt.

I had one setback in my newfound policy of honesty. I was invited to dinner by the president of my company with nine other employees in recognition of our participation in a company-sponsored health program. During dinner, the president's wife asked me if I was married. I told her I wasn't legally married. She nodded her understanding and went on to tell me how, despite her husband's protests, her son had lived with a woman for a period of time, but it was alright now because they had married. She then asked my girlfriend's name. I got very embarrassed and tried to change the subject. She persisted and asked why I wouldn't tell her the name of my girlfriend. By now, we had attracted the attention of the other dinner guests. I was mortified and asked her to stop asking. She ended the conversation by winking and saying that she understood. I have no idea if she really understood. I do know that I felt angry and ashamed that I didn't have the courage to talk about Thaddeus as the other employees at that dinner spoke of their spouses. While I excused myself by acknowledging that I simply didn't feel safe sharing about my life with the company's first lady, I resolved that I would never suppress myself in a similar situation.

In the years that have followed, I have been proud of the many times that I have told the truth despite my discomfort and my fear of possible financial loss. During these times, I have not received one negative comment or reaction to my coming out directly at work. My bosses have all been very supportive of me. In fact, I sense that they have a renewed respect for me and the integrity with which I am living my life. I know I do.

I can't say that I was very thrilled when I first realized I was gay. I can't say that coming out to friends, family, and coworkers has been enjoyable or painless. I also can't say that my life has been easy. But, I can say that I wouldn't change one thing about my life today or my history, since my history is what made me who I am.

I have become a respected colleague in the field of human resource systems, both within and outside of my company, and I expect my career success to continue. Over the years, Thaddeus and I have grown both personally and as a couple, and we have a loving and empowering relationship today. We are approaching our tenth anniversary. Most importantly, I have learned that maintaining my integrity about who I am is the most important thing in my life.

Finally, I have learned that coming out, for me, is a continuous process and I am now out to most everyone in my life. I intend to continue this process to be who I am, and to make the fact of my sexual orientation a matter of public knowledge, free for the asking. I hope that this will enable people to see how very much alike we human beings are, and that we (gays and lesbians) are not to be feared. I hope too that telling my story will help others find the courage to become more accepting and inclusive human beings.

Joe's story shows how making assumptions (as both the president's wife and photographer did) can, inadvertantly, create great stress and discomfort for everyone. Had either used the tools contained within this book (in line with the Do Ask aspect of this book), they would have avoided creating such situations. Joe's story illustrates how gay employees often take such negative experiences and use them to develop positive future actions (the Do Tell aspect).

Joe's story also highlights the fear many sexual minorities face and that causes some to remain closeted throughout their corporate lives. This fear was in evidence in the author's stories and is one that almost every sexual minority faces at some point. The skills and tools that you develop by reading this book will help you create an environment in which sexual minorities can devote less effort to hiding and more to productivity.

**Lisa
Busjahn** Editor

I grew up on a Wisconsin dairy farm during the 50s and 60s. Everyone helped with the farm work—my mother, sister, and I. We worked hard. My parents got up at four o'clock in the morning to milk. Our life revolved around considerations and events such as the size of the milking herd and how early the milk truck was expected to arrive.

When I was old enough to walk, I began following my father to the barn after breakfast. I remember trying to match the wide strides of his shadow on the sand. Sometimes when the morning dampness left the sand moist and bright, I lingered behind to leap and run among his shallow boot tracks. This was a game I loved. I played until the sun dried the sand, or the daily movement of machinery and trucks erased his steps. Then I'd catch up with him. He was huge and could do anything—carry bulging feed sacks above his head, pull calves, lift me into the dark holes and shelves of his tool shed to search for greasy tools. Anything! On the farm my father was God.

During most of my childhood my playground was our farm and the farms of my friends. Until I was five, my days, or as many of them as escaped my mother's protective vigilance, were my own. There were feathers to collect, milkweed parachutes to chase, and a dog or two to follow. Sometimes when my mother became too absorbed in hanging laundry or weeding our garden to keep track of me, I ran the long way down through the bushes and tall grasses to the muddy creek—lured by its dark fascinations: crayfish, snakes, turtles, and sluggish trout.

When I turned six, I went to work with my father on a regular basis. Afternoon milking began around four p.m. In late afternoon, a barn becomes heavy with settled aromas—the mowed-grass smell of green hay; must of wide, old, towering beams; the particular smell of corn and oats, a fragrance that almost flies, as if each oat and each kernel were separate and free in the air.

My father worked most of his life. When he was thirteen, he went to work on a farm not too far from his father's land, and had to quit high school. He spent most of the Depression working on road crews, sleeping in gravel trucks, and living off of beans and cookies. His motto was, "You don't work; you don't eat." As a teenager, I dragged, moped, and complained about doing my chores, but I always had food to eat. As a result, I grew up believing in the justice of a healthy person pitching in when work must be done and feeling the love, discipline, and clarity that comes with being part of a family that works to feed itself. I also grew up knowing my father was racist and anti-Jewish. I was exposed to his tirades on many occasions.

We lived within five miles of where my mother was born, twenty from where my father grew up. They each were raised in protected, Protestant farm communities. My mother wanted to educate her children and keep up with the times; she was determined to tell me the whole truth about sex, but it was not an easy topic for her. Growing up on a dairy farm meant that I witnessed animals breeding, although I didn't understand how that related to humans any more than my friends in town did. I asked my mother many questions about how babies are made. Today we joke about how whenever I asked about babies, she would reply that I had good questions, and that someday we would go to the library to get answers together. Of course, we never went.

When my sister went to college, she left behind her treasure trove of books. I loved reading and worked my way through her childhood acquisitions and into the more adult books she brought back from school. When I was thirteen, I began to read *Giovanni's Room* by James Baldwin, a book about a homosexual. Because my mother wanted me to learn and bought me books for my birthday and Christmas, it didn't occur to me that I wouldn't be able to discuss something presented in print with her. In the evenings, we took walks and I talked about everything I read, saw, and heard. My mom patiently listened and seldom made a judgmental remark. One day I mentioned *Giovanni's Room*. It was as if I had dropped a bomb. She completely cut off any discussion and told me I couldn't read the book. I put it back and only read a bit of it now and then, tiring of it quickly. Probably because it was about men.

I had experienced crushes on girls prior to this time, but it was not until my twelfth or thirteenth birthday that I began thinking seriously about what it meant. I had my first crush when I was in third grade. I was very fond of the girl who sat behind me and began what would be my lifelong pursuit of smart women. Julie was a minor love, however. Although she was the brightest in the class, her penmanship was too perfect and her interest in following the rules too compulsive to anchor my heart.

I did not fall deeply in love until the fourth grade, when I met and courted Debby—by singing K-K-K-Katey daily to her when she returned to the school grounds from lunch. Debby was to hold my heart for the next two years and would not have a true rival in terms of depth of feeling until I reached high school. These were the experiences, passions, and mild concerns

I took with me into high school, but when I turned twelve, I was confronted by a more important set of questions.

As I mentioned, my family was Protestant. It was not only mother's desire to be open to new ideas and people, but my Sunday School lessons that let me know my father's racist, anti-Jewish diatribes were wrong. Although I have since converted to Judaism, my *introduction* to ethics began with my mother's attention and love during long walks and many trips to Sunday School. For this reason, it was very hard for me to face up to the fact that I did not want to be confirmed as a Christian.

I had learned—about the same time as my peers—the word "hypocrisy," which, of course, made me smarter than my parents and neighbors, as well as miserable. This self-perceived wisdom caused me to wish often that I could believe in what I had labeled a "Santa Claus God." Oh, to be naive, I would think wistfully. As wise as I thought I was, I did somehow have enough awareness of others to know that if I said half of what was on my mind, it would cause a storm in our kitchen.

I went through the four years of preparation to be confirmed as a Christian, hoping that I would stumble into belief, or that I would find the words to explain my way out of making a commitment to false belief. I just did not believe in the trinity. I came to the conclusion that I could not be confirmed because I didn't believe in Jesus as Messiah, which was frightening because I would let my parents down, and worse, I would have to tell them about it!

I casually mentioned that I didn't believe in Christ. At that, my father came up with a new motto: "As long as you've got your feet under my table, you'll believe what I believe!" His fist slammed the table. He was a man of few gestures and little emotion, so he had my attention. I was confirmed and learned that there is nothing worse than betraying one's own beliefs. I was miserable because I didn't believe what my family, relatives, and friends believed. I was also ashamed because I didn't have the courage to say so.

I continued to read books about religion and philosophy, both fiction and nonfiction. I read most thoroughly the existentialists, transcendentalists, Buddhists, and Jews. I seemed to be drawn to Jewish thought, ethics and action, and especially to the focus of what is good and evil as framed by the Holocaust and the writing of Elie Wiesel. In the fiction of Malamud and Potok, I felt the issues of choice that were raised by the existentialists were answered in a moral context.

I didn't completely understand what that context was, however, and as I entered my sophomore and junior years in college, I became more aware of myself as a woman oppressed by male religion. I recall considering taking a course in Judaism and shuddering. What could I be thinking? I had just shed Christianity; why would I get near an older, more traditional, and undoubtedly—I thought then—more sexist religion? It would be over fifteen years before I would study the religion and its history and make my conversion.

When I left home to go to college, I lived the first year with my sister in Madison, Wisconsin. The University of Wisconsin–Madison (UW–M) was not my first choice of schools—it seemed too big and overwhelming to me, but my kidneys had failed my senior year in high school, so I had to be near UW Hospitals for close follow-up after having a kidney transplant.

My father had wanted to donate one of his kidneys to me, and my mother, although terrified of losing him—her first husband had died when my sister, Arden, was just four—agreed that he should go ahead. I begged them not to let him give me the kidney, but he insisted he wanted to. My father loved me very much and at age sixty, I think he wanted to accomplish something truly heroic, truly meaningful to him and his family. Because of his fear of medicine and dying, it was indeed a heroic desire. There was a problem during the presurgical preparation, and he couldn't give me his kidney. I was very relieved. I feared I would feel guilty about not being able to be who they wanted me to be, or, worse, that I would fail myself again and act like someone I thought they could accept. In fact, the night before my father and I were to go into surgery, he asked me to go down a dark hospital hall with him to pray—a prayer he had learned through an organization he used to justify his racism and anti-Semitism. I went with him because he was about to risk his life; I hated myself, yet there seemed to be no way out.

This all happened during the year that I told Arden about

my sexual orientation. She was the first person I came out to. Before talking to her, I thought about all the events of my adolescent years. I also thought about how she and my parents might say that I wasn't worthy of having received the gift of life through a kidney transplant—which I had received from a woman who had been killed in an auto accident shortly after the attempt with my father failed. I was scared that Arden would be disappointed and disgusted because my feelings for women were so against the rules, and my sister worked so hard to follow rules. It was horrible to imagine my family might not think my life worth saving because I was a lesbian—I remembered my mother telling me to put *Giovanni's Room* back on the shelf.

Arden had been very supportive and loving when I was sick and she took my news well on a personal level, but warned me not to tell my mother, and also said that she thought that lesbians shouldn't have children. Having children had never entered my mind, but I thought lesbians could probably raise children as well as anyone, and that maybe my sister was not as accepting as she stated.

When I told my mother I love women, she seemed stunned. We argued and spent the next seven years raising and burying the issue at dinners, in hospitals, during walks and in the car. Finally after all those years of living with each other in disagreement and yet as family members, we came to realize my sexuality mattered less than either of us had imagined. We were still a family.

I "outed" myself at work and that too seemed natural. I was a psychiatric aide on the graveyard shift. Often there were only two of us—an aide and a registered nurse—and we handled thirty patients. We had the only locked ward in town and frequently admitted violent males who were in some state of building toward an angry eruption. This meant that one really had to trust the other staff person on the floor to keep a cool head.

The kind of stress these situations created was accompanied by boredom; most nights nothing happened. When I spent eight hours essentially doing nothing with another person I knew I might need to depend on in difficult situations, becoming personal and honest was no tough trick. The staff became very close. I was on the night shift permanently.

I chose to come out to a new-grad registered nurse. Carol seemed pretty sharp. While I had never heard her espouse the old Freudian line that homosexuality was a sickness, I was still a little nervous about coming out because of the horror stories I had heard from other lesbians about coming out to a friend or to co-workers who proceeded to panic, assuming that they were about to be raped. I was also conscious of an underlying belief by men contained in the book, *Women and Madness*, that most of our attitudes and actions are crazy and dangerous. Coming out on a psych ward had its own "thrill," albeit a thrill that was short lived. In fact, it soon became boring coming out to each successive night nurse.

My experiences in coming out at work were positive until I changed careers. Then, I met Mary, who became my supervisor when I moved to Champaign, Illinois, and began work as an editor with a sports and fitness publishing company. Mary was in the process of becoming a fundamentalist Christian. Yet, she seemed openly interested in knowing lesbian women, and even courted me and other lesbians as friends. However, the more she became enmeshed in her new religion, the more intolerant she became. Mary was soon spouting her notions about homosexuality as a sin. She also began to make anti-Jewish comments.

Mary regularly spoke about her beliefs that Jews are stingy, pushy, and not "above board." I felt defensive and very uncomfortable. Although I had not yet converted to Judaism, I was in a process of reading and studying that would compel me to make that choice. Her remarks were hateful and stupid, yet, because I recognized she was ignorant, I thought the best way of dealing with the situation was to quietly and gently guide her to learn more about these issues and let go of her prejudices.

One day she appeared in my office red-faced, literally spitting anti-Jewish statements. Mary had just had a major difference of opinion with one of her authors who was Jewish. I asked her to leave my office. Later, she tried to laugh it off and begin a friendly dialogue with me by saying, "I didn't mean that. I was just joking." We had it out. I felt good about standing up for my beliefs.

A few years later, I worked in a company that created continuing education materials for pharmacists. A gay employee I knew talked to the bosses about having AIDS. The bosses told him that they had no problem with his condition. However, they knew I was taking immuno-suppressants because of my kidney transplant so they wanted to talk to me. They asked if I would be worried about working with someone who had AIDS. I said I had no hesitations about working with a co-worker with AIDS and explained that as a lesbian, I had started writing about AIDS in community newsletters in the early 1980s. At this, I detected a shift in their attitudes, but I wrote it off as just my imagination. "After all, how could they feel okay about a gay man with AIDS and not a lesbian woman?" I thought. The meeting was abruptly ended. The bosses rushed out the door to get a cup of coffee, which seemed odd, considering there was a fairly nice coffee set-up in the office.

Soon, I was hounded by my immediate supervisor. Ron ripped apart everything I wrote, claiming this fact was misrepresented, that sentence was awkward, this comma was misplaced. He'd harangue in this way for two to three hours each morning. In the afternoon I would implement his changes. The next morning he would browbeat me again, contradicting much of what he'd told me the day before.

My desk was in a cubicle next to his office, and when we were finished discussing the material, he would go into his office and open and slam his desk drawers, expressing considerable anger. I had no intentions of quitting my job, so I took his abuse.

Soon, I learned from another gay man in the company that my coworker with AIDS had, in fact, not come out. During his talk with the bosses, he had said that he had foolishly experimented with drugs when he was a young kid, inferring that his was not a gay-related infection. A gay coworker (who was also not out) said that the president told him, "Lisa won't be here much longer because her personal life and politics interfere with her work."

Eventually, I was summoned into the president's office. He asked, "How do you like working here?" "Fine, I like it fine," I responded. He sighed and looked at his desk top. Eventually he said, "Things just aren't working out." Again, he sighed and we waited. Finally, he said, "I don't think you'll be working here any more." I asked if he was saying I was fired. He said, "I guess you could say that."

I was outraged and went to the city with a discrimination complaint against the firm. To my disbelief, it was denied. Even though the president of the company admitted to the investigator that he had said what my gay coworker was willing to testify to, he claimed he hadn't meant it and, besides, that was not why I was fired. He said I was fired for incompetence.

I asked the investigator to explain how the company that had a satisfactory freelance relationship with me for six months prior to hiring me to work full-time and had published two sets of materials I had finished for them, would suddenly have so many problems with me immediately after finding out about my sexual orientation. The investigator said in a meeting she had with me—with a city attorney present—I could make an appeal to the full human rights board.

I decided to take the case to the board because I knew I had suffered discrimination. Furthermore, the city had found discrimination existed in recent cases of two male homosexuals. Even though no case had been found for a lesbian, I was encouraged by their success. However, shortly after I lost my job, my mother called to say my father was dying of lymphoma. The months of listening to my supervisor yell and badger and slam drawers had taken a toll on me and with the fears I had about the process my family was about to go through, I decided not to go through with the appeal.

I write about these two stories together—the anti-Jewish and anti-lesbian experiences—because, to some extent, I think I played a role in the first situation that was similar to the roles my two closeted co-workers played in the second. At the publishing company, there was a Jewish publication director named Sarah who was above both me and my boss, and although I tried to distance myself from my immediate supervisor and squelched the "little" humiliations she tried to perpetrate against Sarah, I didn't speak about my feelings about what she said. I didn't tell anyone who could have changed the situation about the bigotry. I hated discrimination of any kind, yet it was not until Mary became so hateful and it was impossible to ignore her venom that I was able to speak out clearly.

A similar dynamic occurred between the closeted men and me at my next job. They didn't have to come out to express outrage, yet they didn't speak out clearly to the perpetrators of discrimination about their anger and disgust. I believe that until we all begin to look at each other—Jews, homosexuals, people of color, women, people with disabilities—as human beings, precious for ourselves, we will be threatened by the brutal hatred of ignorant people. Now, when I am in situations where people are speaking hatefully or without kindness or insight about a group or a person, I remember the quotation attributed to Reverend Martin Niemoller and try to respond in a way that makes a difference.

First they came for the Jews and I did not speak out...because I was not a Jew. Then they came for the Communists...and I did not speak out because I was not a Communist. Then they came for the trade unionists...and I did not speak out because I was not a trade unionist. Then they came for me...and there was no one to speak out for me.

In her story, Lisa tells of being fired as a result of revealing her sexual orientation—something she did in support of another employee. Her story demonstrates the abundant energy it takes for sexual minorities who do come out under adverse conditions to protect themselves and be treated fairly. Her story tells readers why so many in the sexual minority community chose to use thier considerable energy and effort to hide rather than come out. More importantly, her story speaks to the critical need for each of us to stand up for one another, despite our differences.

Frederick "Rico" Hewitt-Cruz

Medical Laboratory Technician

I was born in Belize (formerly British Honduras), where I spent the first five years of my life. My family moved to the deep South, where I grew up in Oakman, Alabama, a small town about forty miles from Birmingham. I do not know what precipitated our move to Alabama, nor did anyone ever discuss why we moved. Our life in Belize was never mentioned. I know there is more to this story than I have been told.

My father worked in the coal mines, which in that area of the country was considered a very good job. Several of my uncles also worked in the mines. I remember my father as a fairly innocuous man. Occasionally, he would tell me that I was a "good boy" when I did well in school, but generally he said little. He had problems with drinking and he was abusive to my mother though he never physically harmed me. My mother was a very strong woman, whose job was to take care of the family.

As a child, I was always well dressed and was clean and neat. I was known as the "pretty boy." I had long hair, smooth chocolate skin and extra long eyelashes. I looked and acted like a girl. In elementary school, there was a traditional boys' beauty contest in which the boys dressed up as girls. I always won the competition. Soon, I became known as the town sissy. I was called "Miss Freddy." For many years I did not understand what it meant to be a "sissy" or a "fag." I had several sexual experiences with boys who were a few years older than I (they were twelve or thirteen), and I simply thought that I was playing "mommy and daddy" with the other boys.

I did well in school. In fact, studies came easily, almost naturally. There were only a few black students at my school, and it was considered unusual for a black student to do well. Eventually, I was put in a gifted class in which I was the only black child.

When I was twelve, my parents divorced. My father's drinking had become too much for my mother to handle. He had stopped working and became abusive and violent towards her. I recall waking in the middle of one night to shouting voices, dishes breaking, and glasses smashing. My sister and I ran to our mother's room and climbed into her bed. The next morning we awoke to see the house torn apart. And, there was blood. My mother was silent. My father was injured from stab wounds to his hand and arm. I asked mother if she was okay and she said, "I'm okay my children; now, get ready for school." Nothing else was said.

Within less than two years my mother remarried. My new stepfather, who had been a truck driver, became a minister in the Church of Christ. He often told me that I acted like a girl. He was much more confrontational and more of an authority figure than my father. I was very afraid of him. My mother seemed to become a weaker person in his presence, and this dismayed me. I developed a great deal of resentment towards my stepfather.

At school, I was increasingly ostracized and left out of social activities. The teachers, however, seemed to like me, probably because I was such a good student. My stepfather often told me that I must continue to do well in school because I was a minority, but his constant ridicule about how I "acted like a girl" caused me such anxiety that my performance in school began to deteriorate.

Things only got worse when I hit puberty. I started to wear makeup foundation to cover acne scars that I developed. This only made me look more like a girl. When I was fourteen, my stepfather confronted me about my sexuality. He said, "Freddy, I don't know why you won't talk to me and tell me what your problem is, but if you don't, *I'll* tell you what your problem is." My heart began to beat fast and tears rolled down my face. My stepfather got my mother and the three of us talked for hours. I told them that for a very long time I had been sexually attracted to boys. I explained that I had tried to change. I even looked at pornography of women in hopes of making myself straight. I had prayed to God to help me, but nothing happened. My parents were very attentive. They listened with great care. After I finished talking, my stepfather said, "I knew that all along, son." We finally reached an agreement that I would go see a counselor, which I did. That didn't work. I tried going to church more, dedicating "my life to God." "God will fix me; He will change me," I thought. That didn't work. Thinking I wasn't trying hard enough, I read my Bible *more*. I prayed *more*. Nothing happened. I stopped wearing make-up. I cut my long, beautiful hair. I started to wear loose clothes. I actually *acted* like a boy. Nothing changed. I was still attracted to boys.

I began to have "slips," whereby I would have sex with a boy and then repent. I resumed putting on make-up, lightly at first, then with a more heavy hand. Losing any hope of becoming straight, I was soon back to my old ways, which angered my parents. They began to verbally attack me, especially my mother. "You like them boys sticking their things up you," she said with a mean spirit. These attacks would be followed by weeks of silence.

Eventually, I gave up entirely. I was tired! I tried everything I knew to change. "Maybe God wants me to be just like I am,"

I said to myself. So, I went about living my life as a gay man, despite the abuse. And, there was much of it, and not all of it from my family. Several of the older kids and adults began to sexually abuse me. An older girl toyed with me sexually. The father of a friend of mine began to call me a sissy, and then proceeded to coerce me into performing a sexual act with him. He said I was so pretty that I should be a girl, then he would turn around and tell me that if I were a girl, I wouldn't be as pretty. This activity went on for some time. All the while, he presented himself to the community as a straight married man. People began to abuse my sister, asking her questions about me. Soon, she developed migraines.

I felt as if I had put a stigma on my entire family. So, I tried God and church once again. I prayed again and again. I repented again and again. And, I was "saved" again and again. I had up to three and four ministers standing over me praying that my soul would not be damned to hell. NOTHING!

I was known all over town and within a fifteen mile radius as that "black faggot" in Oakman. I couldn't walk down the street without being called queer; nor move through the school hallways without being pointed at or whispered about. The pressure of being called the town queer made my life very difficult. I started dating a girl in a desperate attempt to change that perception, but it didn't work.

During my junior year, I met a "pretty white boy." He was essentially a white version of me. We became friends, and for almost a year we had a strong and intimate sexual relationship. However, the town began to talk about us and no one liked that a black sissy was with a white guy. Soon, my friend began to hate me because of the talk around town and shortly thereafter our friendship ended. I was deeply saddened. People continued to call me a fag. In an attempt to inoculate myself from the pain, I would respond with, "Yeah, I'm the best one I know."

Thanks to my academic performance, I was the first recipient of a scholarship given to a black student by my school. I was very proud, but two days before graduation the principal called me into his office and told me that I would not be able to walk across the stage at graduation to accept the scholarship. He said that there had been several threats made on my life. Because graduation was to be held outside, he thought it would be better for me not to participate, for fear that something might happen. I still received the scholarship but I was crushed by the experience.

Around the same time, another devastating experience occurred. Since my stepfather's entry into the ministry, I had stayed active in his church. I sang regularly with the choir and often sang solos in church and at weddings and other social events. One Sunday, my father invited a guest minister to preach to the congregation. He began to speak of the "abomination of homosexuality." The congregation seemed very still. I could hear my heart beat. Suddenly, he called my name and asked me to come forward. I was told to stand in front of the entire congregation. I was dressed flamboyantly. I looked up and saw my mother and stepfather sitting quietly, their faces expressionless. I knew the names of every person in that church and, in front of these silent people, I listened to this visiting minister attack me. He told me that my homosexuality was the work of the devil and that I would burn in hell if I did not change my ways. He shouted "Repent and beg forgiveness." In my terror and shame, I begged repentance, I begged forgiveness, and I promised to alter my ways. In a way, I was grateful, for I believed every word spoken that day, including the promise that I would be cured. After the service, not one person said a word, although I sensed that many people felt sorry for me. I went home. My parents were sitting in the living room. As I entered the house, they just looked at me. They remained absolutely silent. I was in great pain. It hurt that they offered no comfort after such an enormous public humiliation. I swore I would never again stand in front of a congregation, and I quit singing.

I decided to go to Pennsylvania to see my biological father, who was ill. He had only seen me once for a brief period since he had left six years earlier. When he became aware that I was gay, he shunned me. Feeling abandoned, I joined the Navy in order to escape my family and the pain associated with Alabama and, then, Pennsylvania.

For some reason, I thought that the Navy would make me straight. In the beginning of my Navy career, I was not sexually active. I simply focused on being a good sailor. Several individuals made passes at me, but I ignored them. I had joined the Navy with the hope of becoming straight. I was in boot camp in Great Lakes, Illinois, where our every move was monitored. I was terrified of doing anything anyway. During the second month of boot camp a guy came up to me and told me he knew a place were we could go. My loneliness for another gay man bested my fear and we met. Afterwards, I cried the entire night because the illusion that the Navy would make me straight had been shattered.

The company commander at Great Lakes liked me and called me in to say that he was sending me to corpsmen school in San Diego where I would work in the medical division of the Navy. When I arrived in San Diego I noticed that my class was full of effeminate men and "sissies." I then realized that, in the Navy, being a Corpsman meant you were likely to be gay. My company commander must have suspected me.

My hair was short but I still looked liked a girl. But no one teased me and I established some friendships with other corpsmen who were obviously gay. After a few weeks in training, a lieutenant commander called me into her office and told me that she really liked me but noticed that I appeared to be somewhat effeminate. She said that it did not bother her but that it might bother others so she suggested that I be careful. She was rumored to be a lesbian and it was clear that she did like me, so I started working on being more butch.

While stationed in San Diego, I had met a civilian who worked for the Navy and was a friend of a friend. She was Puerto Rican and I thought she was incredibly beautiful. She was thirty-six years old but looked twenty-one, which was my age. She had been recently divorced, after a marriage of fourteen years. She also had a female lover. By now, I had become sexually active with other men. Neither of our sexual lives were an issue for the other. The fact that we both had a homosexual orientation just added to the growing friendship that we developed. In 1988, we decided to marry. In some respects, it was a marriage of convenience. She received a dependent card (her lover was in the military), and I received slightly higher pay for being married. But we had not married solely for the benefits. We cared for each other and had an incredibly good time together.

This was a very positive time of my life. My "wife" helped me to see life differently. We never did have sex, but we had a tremendous friendship. She had two brothers who were gay, and her family was very accepting about that. And they really liked me. It felt good to belong to a family that accepted me for who I was.

My family reacted somewhat differently. My sister was bothered by the fact that I had married a "white" woman. My parents simply wanted to know when they could meet her. They were probably pleased that I married. I don't know.

In October 1989, I moved to Texas to attend lab school and my wife moved to Virginia Beach with her lover. As I often spoke of my wife, I was perceived as straight but very open-minded, since I would go out dancing at gay clubs. At about this time, Perry Watkins came out after sixteen years in the service. He was discharged but then reinstated because it was shown that no one had asked him if he were gay when he joined. This was a heartening piece of news for me and other gays in the service and I felt safer, though not safe enough to come out, as I knew this issue wasn't "put to bed." So I stayed in the military closet. Fortunately, I still had my marriage to protect me. While Miriam and I are still legally married, we have had little contact since San Diego.

After attending lab school in Texas, I returned to San Diego and was called to serve in Desert Storm. I was in Saudi Arabia from August 1990 to March 1991 and worked in a medical unit about twenty-five miles from the front. At one point, we had something of a cultural exchange with servicemen from Britain who joined our unit. It soon became clear that one of the British guys was gay and he was ostracized. Space was tight and one had to give up on any thoughts of sex while in this situation. It was a long seven months.

Shortly after Desert Storm ended, I decided to fly home to see my parents. I was ill-prepared for the surprise that awaited me. I flew into Birmingham and then we drove the forty-five minutes to Oakman. As we approached Oakman, hundreds of people lined the main road holding signs and American flags. I couldn't imagine what they were doing. Then, I realized that they were waving to me and were shouting, "Welcome home." I was confused. I wondered how this town that had so abused and ostracized me could now be honoring me.

We drove on to the town square where there were even more people. The mayor and members of the city council were there, as was a local representative of the National Guard who presented me with an American flag. The mayor announced that the town was having a dinner in my honor at a "restored" Southern town just outside Oakman. The town was a commercial venture something like "Dollywood." The event was like a local fair, with carnival booths, rides, and games, as well as crafts and women in aprons and bonnets cooking hominy in large pots. On the stage, the mayor introduced me as an alumni of the local high school (the one where I was not allowed to attend the graduation ceremony—no mention was made of that). I was asked to say a few words. I said I was glad to be back and thanked them for the support they had given me and others through their cards and letters. Then I added, "We, the American people, have shown the participants of Desert Storm that we know how to come together despite race, despite color, and despite our other differences. And I hope things will continue that way now that Desert Storm is over." For a moment, there was an awkward silence, then applause. The children of the town followed me by singing a number of patriotic songs. My mother said that she and my stepfather were very proud of me.

Following the songs, I mingled among the crowd. It had been four years since I left Oakman. I knew most of the people at the event and many acknowledged me personally. Some avoided me. I acted like a politician, diplomatically shaking hands and paying particular attention to the children. I was amused by the children and how they would respond when I asked if that sign was for me. With big smiles, they would say, "Yes." I felt like a celebrity. I also felt a strange mix of pride and resentment. I knew that behind all the pretense much hatred and prejudice remained.

After the "event," my mother told me that the church had initiated the plan to honor me. During Desert Storm, I banked all my earnings and sent some of it to some of the people back home. I sent a few checks to my grandmother, a woman on our street, and some others who I sensed might be in need. I did not intend for these actions to be public knowledge. My mother told me that on one Sunday during Desert Storm, the woman to whom I had sent fifty dollars got up and spoke about me. She said that here I was at war yet I didn't act like I was the one in need of support. She said that the money came at a critical moment for her. She also recounted how I had been the choir director, had sung in the church and done a number of other things and that I had probably been hurt in the church as well. After she spoke, my grandmother stood up and said, "And he sent me a check for one hundred dollars." As my mother told me this, I felt like crying as this woman to whom I had sent money was the first person to ever acknowledge my hurt, and I appreciated her acknowledgement.

After my four years were up, I left the Navy in October of 1991 and entered the workforce as a health care professional. Today, I work as a lab technician at a major health center and plan to continue my studies to become a physician. I still live with pain. I probably always will. But, I don't regret the past, for I know that it has led me to where I am today. I freely acknowledge that my inner desire is to be with another man, and I don't think it has anything to do with my hypothalamus or any other thalamus. The reason why I am gay doesn't matter. God knows why I am gay and that's all that matters. My folks have made great progress accepting me just as I am. My mother recently said to me, "All I know is that I carried you for nine months and gave birth to you. God made you and God don't make mistakes!"

On June 27, 1993, after many years of hard work, I finally stood up in front of the entire congregation of my church and said, "I am a proud, twenty-six-year-old African American gay man."

Rico's story demonstrates the cruelty of overt discrimination and the triumph of human spirit over adversity as he goes on to prosper in the U.S. Navy and the medical field. Almost all sexual minorities can relate to such a story—even if they did not actually experience overt discrimination. Managers who make efforts to include all employees are likely to find that their gay, lesbian, and bisexual employees are willing to expend great effort to support the managers' and the organizations' goals and objectives.

Rico's story also illuminates how a large organization like the U.S. Navy targeted sexual minorities for certain positions. Although Rico found work that he enjoys and excels at, a policy (generally unwritten) of pigeonholing certain groups is likely to deprive an organization of realizing the full potential of all their employees.

Jillaine Smith   Administrator: Nonprofit

I am the fourth child of my parents. They grew up in the depression in upstate New York. After World War II my father, recently finished with medical school, brought his young wife and my oldest sister to California where they had three more children. They were thirty-five when they had me. Dad was in the middle of a major career change that ultimately led him to become the head of a key department at a prestigious southern California clinic.

While I grew up in an upper-class environment, my parents never really joined the establishment. I perceived them as social loners, and believe I took that role on myself, never quite fitting in to any particular clique or group. My siblings, significantly older than me, were mostly out of the house by the time I reached adolescence.

As a youngster, I don't remember learning anything about homosexuality. Later, I learned that my parents knew a couple of homosexuals, but they never mentioned or discussed them. At worst, my parents kept me from much knowledge of homosexuality. But, if that is true, then it's also true that they never instilled in me any intolerance of it. Bias does exist in my family, however. My dad is fairly conservative with little patience for people who break the law. Sometimes he lumps certain races into stereotypical groups. But I never felt his racism was very deep. I think he's too intelligent for serious racism. There were certainly racist, sexist, and later, homophobic jokes in our household, but we (my mother and my sisters) always gave him, and then my brother, a hard time for such jokes.

I was eleven or twelve when I first met a homosexual, or at least perceived him to be at the time. He was my friend's younger brother, then six or seven. He was very effeminate and, in the end, my young perception was accurate: he is now a gay man. In high school, I learned that a male friend of my older boyfriend was gay. We socialized and he would sometimes bring a lover to parties I attended. I don't recall any judgment, probably nothing more than curiosity.

I figured that one or two of my physical education teachers were gay but I didn't give it any serious thought. The first lesbian I actually knew was a girl I'd known from a church youth group. Bonnie was a year older than me and very religious. I perceived her as matronly, especially in the way she dressed. I thought she would make a good mother. Bonnie came back from her first year at a midwest college with another girl, and was quite changed. Her hair was long and down in her face and she wore baggy jeans and loose shirts. It was 1976 and she was a "hippie" and was quite "out" as a lesbian. I remember being shocked, not so much because she was a lesbian but how such a strongly religious woman was able to come to terms with a sexual choice (that was how I saw it then—a choice) so contrary to her upbringing. I remember feeling worried for her. But I never knew her as a lesbian, never talked with her after that time as she went back to college and I never saw her again.

I've often wondered what became of her.

In college, I met bisexual women. I even met a cross-dresser. I have no recollection of feeling anything other than curiosity and excitement. I wondered and fantasized about sexual experiences with other women and I even flirted with the only lesbian I knew (in college), but I never perceived myself as anything other than happily heterosexual—that is, until my mid-twenties, when I fell head over heels in love with Betty, a colleague of mine.

Betty, who resisted my affections because I was a "straight girl," identified then as bisexual with a preference for women. I introduced her to my lesbian friend and watched their fire grow and grow, ever envious, wanting that for myself. Later, I did convince Betty of my desire to pursue being lovers with her and we spent most of the next seven years of our lives together. Sometimes, I think I spent most of it trying to convince her of the desire I had for her. I learned a lot about myself during this time, about alcoholism and about codependency. I now have a lot of compassion and sadness for both of us. Since our breakup three years ago, I have been with both men and women. I have even tried a threesome, seeking to meet both sides of my sexual and emotional needs.

While technically I consider myself to be bisexual, I hesitate to use that or any label. I have never felt political about my sexual orientation. I have always felt, since loving a woman for the first time, that my attraction is to *people*, particular people, not just their gender. I've heard and participated in many discussions about bisexuality—none of the typical viewpoints ring true for me. I don't believe that I'm indecisive. I don't believe I "return to men" for social privilege. If anything, I was more uncomfortable when I started seeing men again. I'm also not a bisexual activist. I don't feel any need to go to support groups or march in bisexual contingents in parades.

The only time I felt "righteous" political anger was when a gay twelve-step conference I had attended for years curtailed its bisexual workshops, excluding bisexuals from any active role or representation. I have felt much more prejudice and lack of acceptance from gays than from heterosexuals. And I find myself appalled when I see people who fight against their own oppression then turn around and oppress another group of people. To me, that is the watermark of hypocrisy—using the very weapons of your oppressors to oppress others.

I never performed the "coming out" experience with my family. I simply became "out." I never said, "I'm lovers with Betty," but I included references to her in normal conversation, just as I would about a male lover in my life. I acted as if it was normal and ordinary to spend so much time with this woman. It became known and understood that Betty and I were lovers. Ironically, the first family member to realize the nature of my relationship with Betty was my (then) fifteen-year-old niece, who quite perceptively picked up on the emotions I harbored for this female colleague of mine. Very early in our relationship, I left town rather quickly to return to San Diego where Betty was going through a very difficult time. "That was odd," my sister commented to her teenage daughter, who replied, "Looks to me like Jillaine and Betty are much more than 'friends.'" She was right.

With my family, I initially experienced a fear of rejection. But this faded after a while, especially after the first Christmas that Betty joined the family festivities. If my family had any judgments, they kept them to themselves or to each other. I think that any concerns they might have had had more to do with the emotional dynamics of our relationship than about Betty's gender.

Most of my friends' reactions were positive. Many of my female friends' first reactions were wondering if I had ever felt "that way" towards them. Sometimes I got the impression they were disappointed in my negative answer! In one case, when a former classmate of mine, who expressed an attraction to me, learned I lived with a woman, he said, "Well, I guess I prefer hearing that than hearing you're with a man." The comment didn't sink in until much later when I realized he perceived relationships between women as not serious enough to damage his efforts at winning my attentions. In his eyes, I was still "available." Most of my straight male friends were titillated—as if my newfound orientation offered the possibility of expanded sexual experiences for THEM (threesomes). Only one female friend couldn't "deal with it." Her initial reaction was, "Oh

God, my husband isn't going to like this." We fell away for several years, but today she is much more accepting and even curious. I think all of my female friends were drawn to consider their own level of attraction for other women.

On one occasion, I did make a conscious choice to stay "in the closet." Early in my relationship with Betty, I met an old childhood friend for lunch. We hadn't seen each other in years, but I had always felt an intimate bond with her. At lunch, she told me of her newfound faith in a charismatic Catholic sect. Every word out of her mouth was about the importance of God and religion in her life. At the time, I was strongly biased against any organized religion, especially one that had somehow managed to convert this woman who *looked* like my old friend into someone so unrecognizable internally. I spent most of the lunch weeping, experiencing her change as a loss to me, unable to accept it as a gift in her life.

And I was unable (or unwilling) to increase the gap between us by admitting my own newfound identity. I was afraid of losing even more of this old friend by having her judgment (which I was sure would be there) thrown at me. I saw her again quite recently. We spent the afternoon together. She is still quite religious, but I am less critical. However, I was still unable to tell her of my years living with and loving a woman. For some reason, I felt the need to protect those memories and feelings from someone I was sure would judge them negatively although now I'm not so sure she would do so.

In other areas of my life, I was mostly out from the beginning and especially after we moved to San Francisco. In "the city," I met many lesbians and gays and I heard many "in the closet" and "coming out" stories. And, I heard horror stories of discrimination. I could never relate to them as I have never perceived myself as experiencing discrimination at work or elsewhere. My girlfriend was beaten up for her orientation but I have not directly experienced discrimination or violence against myself.

In my work, I practiced what I did in the other areas of my life—I never made a big deal about my orientation. I simply incorporated my lover into my life. I "became" out. I know this is going to sound arrogant, but I believe that, at some level, I convey a self-acceptance and self-esteem, a competence and intelligence to which people respond favorably. My sexual orientation is just one more aspect of me and not my entire identity.

When I fell in love with Betty, we were colleagues in an academic department at the University of California. Our co-workers watched or didn't as our relationship developed. I neither hid nor flaunted my orientation. It was simply a part of who I was.

If I came out at all, it was to myself. I never expected to fall in love with a woman—it was a big surprise to me, but I enjoyed it and revelled in it. I had momentary doubts the first time we had sex, but they passed quickly.

If there is any "message" to my story, it is that I believe that if we develop and express our strengths, we become more well-rounded, balanced human beings with healthier, happier life experiences. We are much more than our sexual orientation or sexual expression. Our sexuality is just one aspect of us—an important aspect—but not our entire identity.

Jillaine's story demonstrates the importance of being aware of and inclusive of *all* employees, of all sexual minorities. She also demonstrates a seemingly casual, yet effective, approach to revealing her sexuality by simply mentioning her current significant other by name—whether male or female. This approach is similar to how Joe now talks about his lover without editing his name or pronouns. Although this approach seems casual, it is important to recognize that arriving at a place where people feel comfortable coming out requires both a solid sense of self-worth and an environment in which physical or psychological threat has been largely removed. The latter is something that a manager who champions an all-inclusive workforce can help create.

Gaining Skill

3

Techniques for Managers

Most of us in business recognize that people will perform successfully if: they are carefully selected; know their jobs and what is expected of them; have adequate tools, knowledge, skills, and training; and receive feedback, recognition, and rewards that reinforce successful performance. These components make up a *performance system*.

If your performance system is inadequate, you *WILL* experience (unnecessary) performance problems. And, when it comes to issues around gays, lesbians, and bisexuals, the performance systems in most organizations are grossly inadequate.

In Chapters 1 and 2, you were given knowledge about gays, lesbians, and bisexuals who have come to terms with their sexuality. In this chapter, you will be introduced to a set of skills to help you implement a successful system of managing performance.

You will discover how to select diversity-sensitive employees and learn what responsiblities employees have and how they are expected to carry out those responsibilities. In addition, you will become equipped to provide feedback, recognition, and rewards that reinforce and strengthen performance. Finally, you will identify whether or not additional training will help you better manage these workplace issues.

HIRING DIVERSITY-SENSITIVE EMPLOYEES

Most organizations are looking for ways to make the workplace more inclusive, as well as more effective. But when it comes to selecting employees today, there is a host of internal and external rules and regulations managers must follow, which often tell you more about what you can't do than what you can do. So, let's look at what you can do to ensure that the employees you select are diversity-sensitive.

First of all, take a look at your company's diversity and selection policies, as well as any list of corporate or organizational values. If your organization doesn't have a diversity policy, use the one showcased in Chapter 5, *Making It Work: Diversity in Action*. Most diversity policies speak to providing an inclusive workplace.

You can conclude that employees are responsible for embracing the organization's diversity policies and values. So, the skillful selecting manager will gather evidence of job candidates' willingness to embrace such values. You can use the following interview dialogue to gather evidence of whether or not job candidates have embraced similar company policies and values within other organizations. Be sure to adhere to your organization's selection guidelines and to government requirements.

Interviewer. *We have a diversity policy that states "We are an all-inclusive organization; we do not accept discrimination of any kind, for any purpose whatsoever. "Can you give me one or more examples where you worked successfully with people of differing ages, ethnicities, abilities, and sexual orientations?*

Job Seeker. An acceptable response might be: *In my last job, I worked on a task force that included two Asians, a Latino, three whites, one of whom was gay, and a disabled person. We represented men and women of all ages, working cohesively to accomplish a common purpose. In fact, we finished our task ahead of schedule.*

An unacceptable response might be: *I really don't think I could work effectively with (gays, lesbians, whites, Latinos, and so on).*

A response requiring a follow-up question might be: *I have worked successfully on many projects with people of every color, race, creed, gender, age, and ability.*

Interviewer. A good follow-up question is: *Can you give me a specific example where you worked successfully with gays and lesbians?*

Evidence of specific success might be: *I worked on a very successful sales campaign where two members of our six-person sales team were lesbians. We worked very well together and included a sales pitch to the gay and lesbian community, which resulted in our being the #1 sales team in the region.*

Interviewer. *One of our company values is teamwork. Can you give me an example of successfully working as a part of a team?*

Job Seeker. An acceptable response might be: *I have always enjoyed working as a part of a team. I prefer that to working on my own. Let me give you an example. I recently participated in a task force that was put together to increase our market share of minority business. I was a part of a ten-person team that represented almost fifteen different diverse groups. I was the only Asian American on the task force. Not only did I bring my unique perspective to the team, I learned from the other fourteen. As a result of some hard work getting to know one another and the various communities we represented, we increased our minority business share two-fold. Additionally, I*

learned a great deal about myself.
It was an exhilirating experience.

An unacceptable response might
be: When it comes down to it, I
like to work alone, unless I'm
leading the team. Then, it doesn't
bother me.

Select employees who are aligned with company diversity policies and organizational values. Specifically ask for examples of working successfully with people of varying sexual orientations. You will increase the likelihood that these employees will carry out their diversity responsibilities (the subject of the following section), and help to create an inclusive workplace.

DEFINING ROLES AND RESPONSIBILITIES

In business, job roles are the crucial link between an organization's purpose statement (mission), its aims and goals, and its performance system. If you expect your business goals to be fully realized, then the individuals you select to fill jobs must clearly know their responsibilities.

Most organizations today have diversity policies based upon the concept of inclusion (valuing all people). They exist because we believe that by including all people, organizations will accomplish more. This makes obvious good sense to any business person. After all, few people will work hard to help an organization accomplish a purpose or task if they feel excluded or unwanted. Yet, in some organizations, that is exactly what happens. Certain groups (often gays and lesbians) are excluded from the diversity mix, and organizations often fail to garner the support of these groups in accomplishing their goals.

The notion of exclusion is the antithesis of what a good diversity policy is intended to accomplish. At best, excluding anybody sends a muddled message about diversity; at worst, it sends the message to all that DIVERSITY IS NOT TRULY VALUED. When any group is excluded from the diversity mix, the organization seldom accomplishes its diversity goals. Individual roles and responsibilities become muddled or unclear.

Unclear roles are a prime cause of performance problems. In many organizations, people really aren't sure what role or responsibility they have when it comes to working with gays, lesbians and bisexuals. In fact, people tend to be unsure of their role in working with anyone who is different from them. So, if you expect your employees to bring your diversity policies and corporate goals to fruition, their roles need to be crystal clear. Let's look at employee responsibilities in this area.

There are two primary responsibilities of employees when it comes to diversity in general, and to gays and lesbians in particular:

> **Employee Responsibility**
> 1 to promote acceptance of all people—gays, lesbians, and bisexuals included—within the organization by aggressively supporting the company's diversity policies, and
> 2 to ensure that no one—gays, lesbians, and bisexuals included—are discriminated against for any reason, whatsoever.

Clarity around roles and responsibilities is key to attaining desired performance results. It is also the basis for establishing performance expectations, our next skill-building subject.

SETTING PERFORMANCE EXPECTATIONS

Performance expectations are statements of what employees are expected to do in areas of job responsibility. As with job roles, clarity around performance expectations is key to attaining desired performance results and to avoiding performance problems. So let's look at the prime expectations of employees in the two responsibility areas identified in the previous section.

Responsibility #1: *to promote acceptance of all people—gays, lesbians, and bisexuals included—within the organization by aggressively supporting the company's diversity policies.*

Performance Expectations

1   Champion an all-inclusive workforce. Do Ask! Do Tell!
2   When interviewing candidates for jobs, let them know that your organization is all-inclusive, including gays, lesbians, and bisexuals.
3   Welcome newly hired sexual minorities into the workplace.
4   Let employees know what their responsibilities and expectations are when it comes to diversity, particularly as it relates to gays, lesbians, and bisexuals.
5   Provide feedback that reinforces and develops behaviors that contribute to making the workplace more inclusive.
6   Recognize and reward employees who are contributing to making the workplace more inclusive.
7   Encourage employees to participate in workshops, classes and other developmental experiences related to this area of diversity.
8   Respond to criticism by referring to your desire to create an all-inclusive workplace.
9   Stand firm in the face of criticism.

Responsibility #2: *to ensure that no one—gays, lesbians, and bisexuals included—is discriminated against for any reason, whatsoever.*

Performance Expectations

1   Let the message ring loud and clear that you will not tolerate even subtle forms of discrimination.
2   Encourage lesbian and gay employees to point out training and business policies and practices that discriminate based upon the sexual orientation of employees and customers.
3   Review on a regular basis employee responsibility not to discriminate.
4   Respond to homophobic jokes and statements by saying, "That's not okay in this organization."
5   Encourage employees to bring harassment or discrimination complaints to you.
6   Refer employees experiencing harassment or discrimination to the proper authorities within the organization.
7   Follow up to ensure that harassment or discrimination cases are being vigorously and fairly pursued.

By establishing clear performance expectations, you increase the likelihood that employees will perform as desired and bring the organizations' diversity policy to life. Clearly established performance expectations also give a basis for you to provide feedback, recognition and rewards. And clear action in these areas will reinforce the development of an all-inclusive workplace.

THREE KEYS: FEEDBACK, RECOGNITION, AND REWARDS

The primary purpose of providing feedback, recognition, and rewards is to sustain and improve performance. In other words, employees who meet or exceed the goals expected of them should receive abundant feedback and recognition, as well as fair and adequate rewards, all of which are intended to reinforce their good performance. Unfortunately, most people receive little or no on-the-job feedback and recognition, and when they do receive feedback it is often ill-conceived and ill-timed. The end result is that performance inevitably deteriorates. Let's explore this more.

When it comes to feedback, most people tend to think in terms of "positive" and "negative." While positive feedback generally reinforces positive performance, negative feedback, often referred to as "constructive criticism," reinforces negative performance. Human beings have a unique ability to "tune out" that which they don't want to hear, and few people relish being criticized. Consequently, negative feedback simply doesn't work.

We like to use the term *motivational feedback* rather than *positive feedback* because the term motivational feedback has no opposite to infer negative feedback. Motivational feedback is any feedback that reinforces or motivates people to perform well. We also use the term *developmental feedback*, which is any feedback that strengthens, develops, or corrects performance. Developmental feedback is vastly different from negative feedback and far more effective at improving performance. It forces the transmitter of feedback into the role of coach rather judge, the role played by anyone sending negative feedback or giving constructive criticism. Let's look at some examples of motivational and developmental feedback.

Motivational Feedback

>> *Your diversity report is excellent. It is well-organized and nicely written. In fact, it is an excellent example of championing an all-inclusive workplace.*

>> *I really liked the way you acknowledged Chris and showed how her volunteer work at the lesbian and gay community center supported her work here with the firm. That was nicely done and showed how an employee's outside efforts sometime have a nice work payoff.*

>> *I wanted to thank you for welcoming John's partner at last night's company dinner. I think you made both John and Jim very comfortable.*

Developmental Feedback

>> *I think your sales presentation would be stronger if you identify the customers you are aiming to attract, specifically, gays, lesbians, and bisexuals.*

>> *Bill, that was a difficult situation you faced. The next time anyone tells a homophobic joke, simply say, "It's not okay to tell jokes like that." That should stop such behavior and will go a long way to help us meet our diversity goals.*

>> *Jane, I'd like you to review the diversity goals with your team quarterly, rather than annually. I think that will help to improve your team's results.*

Most people have been taught to mix positive and negative messages when giving feedback. This is a technique called "sandwiching," which begins by *telling them something good, then telling them something bad, and ends by telling them something good again.* Most people, when they receive both positive and negative feedback at the same time, tend to focus on one and ignore the other. Motivational feedback must be separated from developmental feedback to be effective.

Effective feedback must be specific and timely. Most feedback given today is too general to be of any value to the receiver and often given too late to be of any use. For example, when you hear someone say, "Good job," they could be referring to any number of tasks. When feedback is nonspecific it leaves the receiver wondering what specifically was good about it.

Motivational feedback should be given as soon as the performance has been accomplished. In other words, DO IT NOW! If feedback is delayed, the receiver is often left wondering what the giver is talking about. The most effective time to give developmental feedback is just before a person repeats a performance that can be improved upon or strengthened. For example, if you observed an employee leading a diversity meeting and you identified something requiring improvement, the most effective time to provide that feedback would be just prior to the time the person leads the next diversity meeting, whether that be days, weeks, or even months away. By providing developmental feedback as closely as possible to the next time the performance is likely to be repeated, you increase the likelihood that the feedback will be useful and that performance will be strengthened.

Performance will also be strengthened by providing abundant and frequent motivational feedback. The old adage, "You can't get enough of a good thing" applies to motivational feedback—though not to developmental feedback, which should be given only when necessary to improve performance and should focus on one or two items to be improved. Feedback that is ill-conceived and ill-timed simply doesn't work.

Developing your feedback skills will take practice, but the results will be worth it. The following ground rules will help you.

Ground Rules for Providing Feedback
1 Separate motivational and developmental feedback.
2 Provide motivational feedback immediately following performance.
3 When possible, provide developmental feedback just before the performance is to be repeated.
4 Tie feedback to performance expectations.
5 Let performers know that you believe they will perform well or continue to perform well, as appropriate.
6 Provide motivational feedback in public or in private; provide developmental feedback in PRIVATE ONLY.

These ground rules and principles apply to daily, informal feedback sessions, as well as the more formal quarterly progress reviews and annual performance appraisals, which basically are documented feedback sessions. By strengthening your skills to provide effective motivational and developmental feedback, you will increase the likelihood that you will meet all of your objectives, whether they be related to diversity, performance, or your life outside of work.

Most of the feedback principles also apply to recognition and rewards. Like effective feedback, effective recognition and reward systems will sustain and improve performance. Recognition and rewards should also be given as abundantly and as often as practical. (The list, "101 Ways to Make Your Workplace More Inclusive," in Chapter 5 provides you with actions you can take to recognize and reward employees.) Let's look at the characteristics of effective recognition and rewards.

Characteristics of Effective Recognition and Rewards

1   *Match the recognition and reward to what the other person values*. What is a reward for you may be punishment for someone else, so take the time to discover what the other person values.

2   *Send the right message*. Be sure what you say reinforces good performance. "You did a good job, but…" or "Now that you've completed this, maybe you'll be able to get on with the rest of your work," sends the wrong message. "Thank you for completing this report. It communicates clearly and concisely. The thoughts presented are well-developed and documented" sends the *right* message.

3   *Ensure that the recognition and reward is appropriate to the performance and occasion*. In other words, don't offer someone a new car for a simple, nice deed and don't give an off-hand "thanks" for something that took weeks or months to complete.

4   *Be creative and resourceful*. Too many people fail to recognize and reward others because they don't have the budget, money, time, or resources. Most people will appreciate a kind word, a homemade something-or-other, a thoughtful gesture. Recognition and rewards are limited only by one's resourcefulness and creativity.

5   *Be sincere/genuine.* Recognition and rewards that are given insincerely are spotted instantly by most everyone. They do more harm than good. Be yourself when providing recognition and results.

6   *Give privately anytime, publicly often.* A good rule to follow is to recognize and reward people in a manner that won't embarrass them.

By adopting these characteristics, you can be sure that the recognition and rewards you provide will sustain and improve performance. Effectively providing feedback, plus recognizing and rewarding people for meeting and exceeding expectations, are essential to creating a high-performance, all-inclusive organization, free of any bias.

Going Further Through Training

If you would like to further expand your knowledge and skills in this area, you might consider attending a training program specifically designed to educate and build skills. To help you decide whether or not you require further training in this area, ask yourself the following questions:

1   Am I getting the kind of performance I want from *all* my employees?

2   Do people in my organization talk freely about their sexual orientation without fear of reprisal?

3   Do I feel adequately informed about these issues?

4   Am I skilled at addressing these issues?

5   Do I stand up for all sexual orientations regardless of my own orientation?

6   Do I know how to manage people in my group who make homophobic jokes or comments?

7   Do openly gay, lesbian, and bisexual employees bring their partners to company social events?

8   Am I comfortable talking about my own sexual orientation?

9   Am I comfortable talking about another person's sexual orientation?

10 Am I taking advantage of the large gay and lesbian customer market?

If you answered no to any of the above questions, additional training would probably be beneficial. For a list of consultants who do training in the area of sexual orientation, please refer to Chapter 7, "Finding Resources."

SKILLS IN PRACTICE

Skill development requires patience, practice, and more practice. The selection, job role, performance expectations, feedback, recognition, reward and training tools contained here are intended to help give you real, live, on-the-job practice.

Frankly, the skills you are developing here have application far beyond that of working effectively with people of different sexual orientations. They can be used to help you work with African Americans, Asians, Caucasians, Hispanics, Native American Indians, Pacific Islanders, people with disabilities, females, males, those over fifty, and those under fifty. In other words, the tools and resources contained within this guide, with slight modification, can be used to effectively work with anyone and to produce high-quality business results.

We hope that they will encourage you to continue to develop your skills—and to make the workplace more accepting, more inclusive.

Using Knowledge

4

Stories of Diversity-Sensitive Managers

We now introduce you to three managers who have used their knowledge of, and experiences with, gay coworkers, neighbors, and others to champion an all-inclusive workforce. These are role models for those of you wanting to effectively manage your workgroups. Vince Patton, Ed.D., is an African American and a high-ranking member of the U.S. Coast Guard. His childhood experiences with "Homer the Homo Man" made him aware of the pain and costs of exclusion, as well as the satisfaction and joy one experiences moving to a place of inclusion and acceptance. You will see how he uses these experiences to effectively manage this issue even in a "Don't Ask, Don't Tell" military environment. Dale Barr's story is about a conservative midwesterner who is influenced by two coworkers, one gay man and one woman, and how he ultimately developed these friendships and used them as motivation to become an advocate for gays and lesbians at work. Constance Holmes is a successful management trainer who grew up in one of the few all-black towns in America. She relates her own experiences of prejudice and tells us how these experiences shaped her ability to support all employees.

These three managers are successful leaders in creating an all-inclusive, productive workforce. As you read through their stories and begin to apply the tools contained within this book, you are preparing yourself to join these managers in working to improve the performance of everyone.

**Vincent W.
Patton, III, Ed.D.**   Coast Guard Officer

I was born in 1954 in Detroit, Michigan, and raised in an all-black area of town that was situated between two affluent white sections. Folks referred to it as "Black Bottom," to denote you were at the bottom of the heap. My mother was a nurse, and my father was a career Army man. Surprisingly, I never experienced life as a "military brat," because we stayed in Detroit while my dad did the moving around. It was a somewhat strange but loving relationship between my parents. They got along fine with Dad's never-ending absences. I am the third boy, fifth child of ten children. My parents still joke that the number of children is directly related to the number of times my dad said good-bye when he was off to another assignment.

Because my dad spent a great deal of time away from home and my mother worked full-time, my maternal grandparents, who lived with us, served as surrogate parents. My mother loved her job as a nurse, and it always amazed me how quickly she would get back to work at Henry Ford Hospital after she had given birth to a child, usually within a few weeks. Having the support of her parents made it possible for her to continue her career—which was unusual for a black woman in the 1950s and 1960s, especially for one with a large family.

Growing up in the inner city was a challenge. During my childhood and adolescent years, I witnessed drug deals, violent crimes, and the Detroit riots of 1967. Yet I don't recall living constantly in fear. Back then, everyone knew everyone, and the neighborhoods were sort of an internal urban family. During this time, blacks usually stuck to themselves, and seldom ventured outside of the "hood," as we called it, because that meant leaving our comfort zone, thus our security.

Although I never really considered my family poor or destitute, I knew that the dollar had to be stretched. Hand-me-downs were de rigueur. My biggest luxury was going out once a month to a fast food joint, White Castle, for those "itty-bitty," square, twelve-cent hamburgers, which I could eat in one bite.

My mother and grandparents were God-fearing, church-going people. Ironically, each of them attended a different church. My mother is Catholic, my grandfather Baptist. My grandmother, who had an "avant garde" approach to religion (her expression), preferred the no-nonsense, no-frills, storefront churches and crusade tents that were so popular in the black community in the 50s and 60s.

With such diversified religious backgrounds, I got my fill of the battle between the Baptists, the Catholics, and the "Whatevers" my grandmother followed. After comparing notes, each of us kids decided that Grandmother's church was the liveliest, with deep-rooted black spiritual singing and dancing. Come Sunday morning, all of us wanted to go with Grandma. So as not to offend our mother and grandfather, we would hold a weekly lottery to see who would go where. I always lost and became a Catholic by default. It was twenty years later that I learned that my older siblings had rigged those lotteries so they could get to go with Grandma.

I was educated in the public school system. I was a very good student in elementary and junior high school, getting mostly A's and B's. My good grades got me into the city's only science and arts college-prep high school, Cass Technical. Cass Tech is where big stars such as Diana Ross and Lily Tomlin graduated. Shortly after I started high school, my hormones kicked in and I began to chase girls. While my social life blossomed, my academic success diminished—I did just well enough to get by and keep Mom and Dad happy.

When I was eleven, I frequently ran "errands" for my grandmother. Later, I found these "errands" were actually numbers running (illegal lotteries), which at the time I didn't realize was against the law. It was in fact conducted so openly that even black police officers patrolling the neighborhood usually "played the numbers."

Just a few blocks from where I lived there was a man named Mr. Homer Sylvester. As long as I can remember, the kids and neighbors referred to him as "Homer the Homo Man." I was warned by my entire family never to go by his house and that if I didn't heed this advice, he would get me and do "nasty things" to me. Not fully understanding what those "nasty things" were at eleven years of age, I imagined them to be pretty dreadful. Thus, whenever Mr. Sylvester walked by, I would either walk to the other side of the street or look down or away. There were times I sneaked a glance at him. I thought he looked like a very sad and lonely man. I wanted to ask him why he was called "Homer the Homo Man," and ask him if he was in fact a homo.

One day, my grandmother asked me to run one of her "errands." My grandmother was adamantly against Mr. Sylvester living in the neighborhood, so I was very surprised when she asked me to take some numbers over to him. I later learned that Mr. Sylvester was the backup numbers man in the neighborhood. She gave me at least half a dozen warnings not to go into his house, *and* to take someone with me. Obliging, I stopped by my best friend Marty's and begged him to come along. After accepting my promise of a quarter if he joined me, Marty promptly "wimped out" when Mr. Sylvester came to the door. He tossed the quarter to me saying, "See ya 'round Vinnie, I ain't letting that fag get me!" Then he took off as if he had seen a ghost.

For the first time, I got a good look at Mr. Sylvester. I had imagined a man with a face that was grotesque somehow, perhaps with makeup and lipstick like Little Richard, and with a feminine voice and mannerisms. As Mr. Sylvester opened the door, I saw a man who in his late forties looked no different from any other black man I'd ever seen. He smiled as he opened the screen door, and I heard his voice, which didn't sound remotely feminine. As if he knew I was scared, he kept a safe distance from me, saying, "Hello, Vincent, your grandmother told me that you'd stop by. Let me get those [number] sheets from you, so you can quickly be on your way." As I fumbled in my pocket for little sheets the size of laundry tickets, he could see how nervous I was. I was so scared that I couldn't talk. I handed him the sheets and in doing so noticed how badly my hands were shaking. As I turned to walk away, Mr. Sylvester said with a smile, "Have a nice day. I hope your father's doing well and is safe [my dad was in Vietnam]. I will keep him in my prayers for a safe return. Take care, young man."

As I walked home, my mind was reeling with thoughts of my encounter with Mr. Sylvester. Suddenly, I began to feel really sorry for him. "Imagine that, he's praying for my father," I said to myself. I began to feel bad. My dad was a well-known homophobe in the neighborhood. Whenever he was home, he'd say things like, "Is that queer still hanging around here?" Sometimes he'd say this loud enough for Mr. Sylvester to hear. I truly admired my Dad, so it hadn't taken long for me to emulate him. I had hated Mr. Sylvester, as I did all homosexuals. Hearing Mr. Sylvester say what he had about my father really made me think.

For some reason I couldn't explain, I suddenly turned around and went back to Mr. Sylvester's house. He was surprised to see me. I said, "Mr. Sylvester, I want you to know that I appreciated what you said about my dad. Thank you very much. I also want to tell you how sorry I am for the way I have treated you all these years." Mr. Sylvester seemed stunned. All he could manage to say was a whispered "Thank you." I left for home. A few days later on my way home from school, I saw him walking down the opposite side of the street. This time, I ran across the street—and almost got hit by a car—just so I could walk past him and look him in the eye to say, "Good afternoon, Mr. Sylvester."

As weeks passed, our simple encounter blossomed into a friendship. Eventually, I asked him the ultimate question, "Are you gay?" He replied that he was, and asked me why I was being so nice to him. He said he was concerned for me because other people in the neighborhood, and my friends, might think that he was taking advantage of me. I explained how moved I was by what he had said to me about praying for my father and that I now realized that he, Mr. Sylvester, was no different from anyone else. Also, I told him that I was embarrassed that I had treated him as if he didn't exist and said I was wrong for having hated him for no reason at all. I was ashamed that I had stooped to the level of the racists I had seen on TV during the marches and demonstrations led by Dr. Martin Luther King and I hated myself for contributing to discrimination.

Later that evening, I wrote a letter to my father, and told him about this experience. My older brother begged me not to do it, saying that Dad would "go nuts." He said Dad might even try to kill Mr. Sylvester if he found I was befriending him. Surprisingly, when I got my dad's letter a few weeks later he told me that, as a result of what I told him, he had written to Mr. Sylvester expressing his remorse for acting so badly and saying the many things he did about him. He said to Mr. Sylvester, "Now that I see death every day from people of different hues, it doesn't matter who or what you are. I have to keep reminding myself of that. I'm over here fighting to uphold the Constitution of the United States for all of the George Wallaces of the country. I'm over here ducking bullets to keep folks who call me a 'nigger' free. Somehow, [by the way I treated you] I began to feel that I was no better than the 'nigger' callers."

After that, my mother and grandmother began to befriend Mr. Sylvester as well. I learned from my grandmother that Mr. Sylvester's lover was killed tragically in an accident at the Ford Motor plant. Shortly after the funeral, Mr. Sylvester became seriously ill with pneumonia. My mother, who worked twelve-hour shifts, stopped by his house, and helped nurse him back to health. While the rest of the neighbors continued to turn their backs on him, my mother and grandparents became strong supporters for Mr. Sylvester's civil rights in the "Black Bottom" section of Detroit. My grandfather, who came around to accepting Mr. Sylvester's lifestyle despite his Baptist background, stepped right into the middle of arguments in Mr. River's Barber Shop, avowing that Mr. Sylvester belonged in the neighborhood, "the same as everyone else."

A few years later, Mr. Sylvester died of cancer. I learned he had been a strong advocate for the underground black gay community in Detroit. Nearly one hundred people, mostly gay, turned out for his funeral. My entire family, with the exception of two brothers serving in the military, were also there. My grandmother read the eulogy. As a family, we all agreed that we had lost a dear and close friend. I remember my mom saying, "I feel like I lost my brother."

I was proud of my family, all of whom, in a short period of time, rallied behind Mr. Sylvester. And I was especially proud that I was the one who initiated it. That experience led me to accept and appreciate the differences in all people, and I have stood taller and stronger ever since.

At the age of seventeen, I finished high school and joined the Coast Guard. On the day I left for basic training, I said good-bye to all of my family, friends, and neighbors. Everyone seemed proud of me, especially Dad, who told everyone he saw that I was joining an elite group. He also warned me that the Coast Guard didn't have many blacks in it. I didn't know just how true his words were until I arrived in Cape May, New Jersey, for training. The year was 1972. The only other blacks I saw were a couple of other recruits. I was in the Coast Guard for almost a year before I met my first black Coast Guard officer.

In most groups I was the only black and it was grueling. In my first day of training, the senior instructor told me, "The job of a marine radio operator is to be a quick thinker and clear speaker," adding that he didn't think these were qualities my ethnic group possessed. I became determined to get through the twenty-four week course. Proudly, I graduated at the top of my class.

After radio-operator school, I was assigned to a weather-patrol ship out of New York City at the Coast Guard's largest base, Governor's Island. Unknown to me, just months before my arrival a very serious racial disturbance had taken place, and some black Coast Guardsman were court-martialed for inciting a riot and other offenses. The incident, which stemmed from a fight between a black and a white Coast Guardsmen, turned into a violent outburst in which one white Coast Guard officer was severely beaten when several black members attempted to take over one of the ships. Needless to say, the racial tension was thick.

The blacks didn't get together socially for fear that someone would think we were "up to something." Determined to make the best out of my hitch, I withdrew into myself. To pass the time, I began to take college correspondence courses. After serving two years on board ship, I had earned over sixty college credits. I was on my way to earning a college degree— something I had thought was almost out of reach for me.

My next assignment was Detroit, my hometown. I was very enterprising in the way I carried out my work, switching shifts, working nights—in an effort to continue my college education. Before my four-year enlistment was up, I had earned my Bachelor of Arts Degree from Shaw College in Detroit.

In 1976, I reenlisted and was offered the opportunity to go to Chicago to become a Coast Guard recruiter. I accepted, knowing that I would now have the opportunity to increase the number of African-Americans and other ethnic groups in the Coast Guard. My tour was exciting and I became the most productive recruiter in the Coast Guard. I enrolled in Loyola University's master's program in counseling and graduated in 1978. By now, my Coast Guard career was beginning to take off. I became widely known throughout the service, and my notoriety earned me some exciting opportunities.

I decided to pursue the goal of becoming Master Chief Petty Officer of the Coast Guard, the highest ranking enlisted person in the Coast Guard. My advocacy for civil rights and equal opportunity fueled this goal. I began to pick and choose career assignments carefully. I said "good-bye" to my occupation in marine radio communications and "hello" to the world of human resource management and development.

I reenlisted once again and became the equal opportunity specialist for all Coast Guard units in the Great Lakes region, based in Cleveland, Ohio. This was a highly visible and demanding job. I was responsible for providing sensitivity and human-awareness training to over twenty-four hundred Coast Guard members and for responding to complaints regarding civil rights, fair treatment, and equal opportunity. My passion for people and my interest in diversity was growing.

It was during this assignment that I encountered my first problem with the way gays were treated in the military. Unlike the other military services, the Coast Guard's ban on homosexuals was somewhat loosely worded, which made it confusing to interpret accurately. I decided to put this regulation to the test when a young female Coast Guard member admitted that she was a lesbian to several of her shipmates. Her commander submitted paperwork to discharge her. The letter requesting her discharge indicated that he was "sorry to submit this because her performance was outstanding." As part of standard procedure, such discharge requests were forwarded to my office for review and comment. I surprised my superiors by recommending her retention, explaining that there was no basis for discharge simply because she made an admission. I added that the regulations were so obtuse that one could easily interpret them to mean that you had to observe someone perform an act of sodomy in order to effect a discharge. While I felt I was taking a risk, I just couldn't back off, especially since her performance record was exceptional. Also, in the back of my mind was Mr. Sylvester. The risk paid off. Once the case was reviewed by the legal officers, they essentially agreed with my findings. This young woman is still in the Coast Guard and is highly regarded.

Not too surprisingly, the regulation was soon rewritten to "tighten up" the loophole. It was dubbed "The Patton Amendment," for which I was not too happy to take credit. In the eyes of my superiors, I had done a great job of bringing the loophole to everyone's attention.

In 1981, I became the first enlisted person ever to be selected to complete a special work project while attending graduate school under paid sabbatical. After less than three years, I earned a Doctorate of Education from the American University in Washington, D.C., where I developed a new performance appraisal system. Upon graduation, I remained in Washington for another year in order to implement and evaluate the system. I received much national recognition and earned numerous military and civilian awards for this work. My "fruit salad" (ironically, the name given to the ribbons on my uniform) began to grow.

When I completed this work, I had a strong desire to return to sea, where my work in education and training had started. I wanted to slow down the pace of my life and get back to the mainstream of the Coast Guard, working on the humanitarian missions that interested me when I joined. I moved to Seattle, Washington, in 1986, and for two years I was stationed aboard the Coast Guard Cutter "Boutwell," patrolling the Alaska waters. I was thirty-two. It was the best tour of my career.

I returned to Washington, D.C., in 1988 to Coast Guard Headquarters as a training manager and performance analyst. Five years later, I was promoted to Command Master Chief for the entire Atlantic area, which includes all units east of the Mississippi. I am one short step away from reaching my goal to become the Master Chief Petty Officer of the Coast Guard.

I know now that the more open and willing I am to find out about differences in people, the more tolerant and accepting I become. That's what happened to me and my family. I'm fortunate that I began to learn this lesson at an early age. I remember Mr. Sylvester saying to me, "It's not important what others think of you; what's important is what you think of yourself." As a black, heterosexual male, that's the message I'd like to leave with people, especially my colleagues in the service.

> In Vince's story, we see how his childhood experiences helped prepare him to effectively manage these issues in the military. In particular, we see how Vince (and his entire family) grew to accept and admire "Homer the Homo Man" and through their mutual support found the strength not to worry about what others thought of his or

his family's relationship with Homer. His experience shows that just as sexual minorities seek support from each other on this issue, heterosexuals also look for allies who support their efforts to be inclusive. This is an important point, especially in organizations that are blatantly homophobic. Seeking out others who share your desire to create an environment in which all workers are welcomed and included will help you get past some of the difficulties, such as those Vince faced in his support of the lesbian who was up for discharge. Vince was not deterred by arguments to keep gays and lesbians out of the Armed Forces. Instead, he goes on to find other ways to support an all-inclusive environment.

Dale Barr — Manager

I am a white, middle-aged, conservative, midwestern, Catholic heterosexual male. I have four children ages thirteen to twenty-three and am married to my second wife—a woman that I had known in college and whom I convinced to return to the United States from England to marry me in 1990.

I was brought up in an environment that dictated a very strict code of behavior, as well as preached about the "evil" differences between my environment and the rest of the world. I was born on the day the Roman Catholic Church celebrates the feast day of Saint Blaise. Saint Blaise, the bishop of Nicea, saved a small child choking on a fish bone and the Roman Catholic Church deemed this to be a miracle and canonized Blaise. Subsequently, every February 3rd the Catholic Church blesses the throats of their congregations. This little "miraculous" story gives insight to my childhood value system, as my childhood revolved around the beliefs and customs of the Catholic Church. My mother is a devout Irish Catholic, my English/Irish father is a convert to the Catholic Church from the Methodist Church. Like many other converts, he is more fanatical about following church precepts than those who are born into the church.

My home was in a low-to-middle income neighborhood in Omaha, Nebraska. My childhood values were strongly influenced by midwestern ethics and priorities. Omaha is a town that is divided by race and money. South Omaha is a melting pot of people who are descendants of many European countries. The people in South Omaha work at the packing houses and cattle feed lots. East Omaha is the warehouse district and railroad yards. North Omaha is where the African-American population lives. West Omaha is where the white-collar, affluent people live.

As in most good non-contraceptive Catholic families, my parents had several children. I was the first of seven. As the oldest, I was given the grown-up responsibilities of babysitting, burning the trash (a high-risk job), and punishing my little brothers and sisters if they got out of line. Assuming adult responsibilities at an early age hastened my adult psychological development.

The first time I realized that I was affected by differences and prejudice was when my parents decided to move from our comfortable, safe northeast Omaha neighborhood to West Omaha. I was upset! Why were we moving and why did I have to leave my friends, baseball team, school, and church? I asked what was going on and my parents said we were moving because "colored" people were coming into our neighborhood. They said there was going to be a crime wave, property values would drop, the houses would become run down, and our Catholic parish would lose its status as one of the more prominent parishes in Omaha. "Colored people caused these things to happen" was my parents' testimonial.

I wanted to believe them, but I hadn't seen any colored people in the neighborhood. If they were there why didn't I notice any run-down houses? Why weren't my friends moving? Did I trust my parents' judgment? Did I hold the values they thrust upon me as the oldest child and was the sacrifice of losing my friends justifiable?

Torn by such questions, I confronted my parents. Their rationale seemed weak, and I began to question the truth of what my parents and the church had led me to believe. I consciously began to wonder: Do Jewish people hoard money? Do Protestants swim naked at the YMCA? Are men who dance on TV or in the theater queer? Can priests make mistakes? Was questioning authority wrong? Are women inferior? Is sex bad? I'm sure between the ages of ten and thirteen I was a trial for my parents, although I was never disrespectful.

I continued to be the "man" of the house. For years my father was in insurance sales. He left on Monday mornings and returned on Friday nights. Disciplining my brothers and sisters was my job, delegated to me by my mother. As a result, my siblings and I are somewhat distant since, after all, I was the wicked witch of their childhood.

When we moved to West Omaha, there were no stores, schools, or churches. My parents couldn't enroll me in a Catholic school so I was bused forty-five minutes into an Omaha public school which convinced me that some of my parents' truths were false. I had always been told that Catholic schools were the best. But the public school I went to was terrific. There were art classes, shop classes, and girls with colorful dresses and nylons. There were no dull uniforms and white bobbysocks on the female student body. There were Jews, blacks, Protestants, rich, and poor at the same public school. The teachers were personable, fair, and challenging. I made honors at the public junior high and one of my teachers suggested that I move on to a college preparatory high school to further my education.

I decided to take the admittance test to a Catholic Jesuit college preparatory high school. I asked my Dad for the ten dollars to take the test. I thought he'd love the thought of me going back to a Catholic school. He floored me when he said he had paid taxes all his life for public education and that I should stay in a public school. Determined to go to the Catholic high school, I paid my own test fees and tuition.

During my high school years, my relationship with my parents became distant. I loved my mom and dad but we were never close and we never shared any of the intimate details of our lives. Paying my own way through these years further pushed me into adulthood at an earlier age than most of my peers. I chose my own values and developed my own opinions. I rebelled. I became an activist against the Vietnam War. I marched in civil rights demonstrations and for ten years I supported women and gay causes by donating money to various activist groups although I invested little time, commitment, or heart to those causes. In the late 1970s I met two people who so touched my heart that I began to seriously look at my commitment to these two communities—women and gays. I realized that ten years of sending money wasn't enough.

I had taken a two-year work assignment on the East Coast. I thought of it as the "country boy heads to the big city." In New York, I met a woman who was to be one of my colleagues. I was blindsided by her candor, her ability to confront sexism, and the professional way she conducted business. I had all of the stereotypical notions of women in the work place. But here was a woman who knew who she was, acted like it and made sure no one discriminated against her. This single experience of working with this woman and three of her female peers prompted me to become a more active "feminist." On my return from the east coast, I helped form a women's support group within my corporation. This organization, twelve years later, is still functioning and is as strong as ever.

I also developed a friendship with a gay man named Mike. Our relationship took nurturing and time. Over the years, he fed me small bits of information about the gay community that I consumed and digested until my uninformed fears of the gay community diminished. At the outset of our friendship I knew that I was out of my ordinary "comfort zone." At first I couldn't put my finger on it. Mike openly shared his feelings and spoke with gratitude about our budding friendship. He told me of his own ups and downs with a sincerity and warmth that I had not experienced with my "buds" in Omaha (I know that my friends are genuine, but they have difficulty showing it through expressions of love and commitment to one another). As time passed so did my discomfort.

Mike knew himself, knew what he wanted, and knew what he wouldn't tolerate (much like the woman mentioned above). Mike could hug people. I was never allowed to hug or show affection. These were traits that I admired and aspired to. We worked together for several years. I was unaware of Mike's sexual orientation during the first year. It didn't matter because I was simply trying to develop a friendship with someone I liked and admired.

During the second year of working together I found out that Mike was gay. He did not profess to me he was gay. He simply invited me for dinner to his home where he and his partner lived. I knew that I had truly accepted gays as human beings. Mike and his lover were not freaks. The only difference between us that I could identify was our sexual orientation. I recognized Mike's deep feelings for his partner and was distressed as I thought of the intolerance they face in our culture. Mike and I have now been friends for over fifteen years, and our relationship has grown to where I now consider him one of my brothers. I am proud of our relationship and I can comfortably and openly speak about his sexual orientation.

These experiences have given me a strong desire to get to know about the lives of all the people that I work with, not just what group they belong to or where they came from. I can now see how the experiences of my youth and early adult years have been provocative and insightful for me. I appreciate and understand the difficulties women, gays, people of color, and people with disabilities have in moving public opinion. I understand and realize the fear and shortsightedness of uninformed people regarding people who "seem" different. I recall the years when I was developing my values, when I was questioning everything and the subsequent changes I went through. That searching and development was of great value, for it helped me construct an understanding of who I am, what feelings I possess, the amount of fact I base my opinions on, and the degree of fear I feel in an uninformed situation. And, it has helped me to become a healthier and more accepting human being.

I will always value my friendships with Mike and others and, as a result, I have "upped" my commitment to these causes. While I still contribute money, I also have increased my personal involvement in ending discrimination. For nearly ten years, I have worked for U.S. West Communications in Omaha. In conjunction with my job, I have been a director on the company's diversity council. I strongly advocated giving the company-support-group status to an internal support group for homosexuals called Eagle. This was an extremely controversial issue at U.S. West. However, after much upper-management soul searching, the company officially supported Eagle. While my role in accomplishing this was minor compared to the hard work of many Eagle members, I do believe that it took a few of us straights talking and writing letters to the right people to help move along the process of endorsement. I continue to be a strong supporter of Eagle. I am a straight man who believes in diversity, in equality, and who opposes discrimination of any kind. I hope I can help others become tolerant, accepting of individuals like Mike who have so touched my heart.

Dale's story shows how conservative values can be translated to champion an all-inclusive workforce that includes sexual minorities. In his story, you see how two coworkers (and Dale's openess to developing his relationships with them) provided him with new insights and valued friendships. Dale provides readers with an example of someone who took concrete action to support gay and lesbians at a major telecommunications company. Like Vince Patton, Dale's support grew from his friendships and acquaintances with gay people.

Constance Holmes   Training Director

T here are only seven or eight all-black cities in the United States. Mound Bayou, Mississippi, a rural community of 20,000 located in the Delta, where everybody is black—doctors, policemen, teachers and politicos—is one of them.

I was born in Mound Bayou in 1958, the youngest of eight children. My father, who had a seventh-grade education, was sixty-one years old when I was born. My mother, who also ended her schooling in the seventh grade, was half his age. We were a farming family, and like many black families, very religious.

My father raised soybeans, cotton, and corn. The entire family worked on the farm. Most of my siblings were much older than I, and, given my father's age, he and I generally "supervised" the work the other family members did. We would ride around the farm in my father's pick-up truck. Every once in a while I smile and think that was my preparation for supervising people in my work today.

I idolized my father. He was a well-respected man and very loving. More than anything, he believed that education was the one way for us to make it in the world. I remember him saying to me, "Girl, get your lesson." Because of his beliefs, I and all seven of my brothers and sisters are college educated, a remarkable achievement given that the most my father probably ever made was $10,000 in any given year.

He didn't consider himself poor though, in part because he owned his own land, and partly because in Mississippi in the 1950s one didn't need much money to survive. I'm not sure how he did it, though, as all of his children attended private Catholic school. This was unusual, not simply because of the cost, but because we were devout Baptists. I remember studying catechism from Monday through Friday and singing hymns and participating in church activities during the weekend. I liked church, though I really didn't "get out the Bible" until I was an adult. My favorite activity was participating in the "speeches," which the kids gave at church. I think that was my preparation for my first career as a radio announcer.

Growing up, I spent most of my time with my father or alone. I seldom played; I was the "mature" kid, the one that would help the younger children get started playing and then leave. I liked being around older people, which is true even today. When I wasn't with my father, I read. I seldom watched television. On Sundays, in addition to attending church, I visited my cousins.

The towns adjoining Mound Bayou were racially mixed. My father would take me there twice a year to shop for clothing, the one thing we couldn't buy in Mound Bayou. That is where I first ran into whites and Chinese. The Chinese owned the grocery store and the whites owned the clothing store. I don't recall anything remarkable about seeing different races. In fact, it seemed quite natural.

Ironically, my first taste of discrimination occurred in Mound

Bayou. I was in kindergarten. Even though we were all black, I remember thinking Mrs. Springer liked the lighter-skinned students better, even though I was a better student. It wasn't that I felt singled out; I didn't. But I did feel that I wasn't getting the opportunity to shine because I was darker-skinned.

During most of my growing up, I didn't experience much discrimination and never on a daily basis. I knew that it happened to others, but because our town was all-black and because I so seldom watched television, the extent of prejudice in America was unknown to me. For example, I was about ten when Martin Luther King was killed, and I don't remember the event.

I knew little about homosexuality. It was seldom talked about within the black community. While there were some homosexuals in the community—many worked as nurses in the hospital—I didn't know any of them personally. Nor did I believe that there was anything particularly wrong with homosexuality. I simply didn't think in those terms (right or wrong), that is until a very religious friend pointed out a reference in the Bible and told me that homosexuality was not acceptable. I was left feeling confused. My confusion was compounded by the fact that there were gay musicians in most of the black churches, yet many black preachers spoke of the evils of homosexuality. I didn't understand how either the homosexual or the preacher reconciled these conflicting positions. How a preacher could have someone in his church who was gay and, at the same time, talk about it as a problem, or how homosexuals could subject themselves to such preachings and still go to church simply didn't make sense to me.

I met my first gay person when I was in college. I worked in the hospital with a guy whom I thought was gay. It was just an impression, but I believe now it was accurate. He never said he was gay; in fact, he often talked about having a girlfriend. I never saw him with any girls nor did I really believe that he had a girlfriend.

At Jackson State, a mostly black college in Mississippi, I majored in Radio and Television Communications. When I graduated, I got my first job in radio. My boss saw my talent more than the color of my skin. This was also true in my second job, where my boss used to call me his "black pearl." I did not find this offensive, and when he decided to leave, he offered me a job with his new organization.

The first time I experienced blatant racism was when I was working on an internship program. My roommate was a white woman. The person next door used to play her radio very loudly. My roommate would usually go next door and ask her to turn it down. One day, however, she asked me to do it. So, I knocked on door of the apartment. I could hear the woman approaching when I heard a man's voice say, "I betcha that's the police." The woman looked at me through the peephole and I heard her say, "Oh no, that's just the nigger next door." She opened the door and I told her what I wanted. She was polite, but I was hurt and somewhat concerned about my safety. I wondered if this was how all whites really felt.

In 1980, I entered graduate school, where I majored in Instructional Design. I was the only African American in the program. In 1982, I began to work as an intern at Arthur Andersen in St. Charles, Illinois.

St. Charles, like the graduate school I attended, is almost entirely white. For the first couple of years I felt as if I was giving up my life for my career. I hardly had any black friends and there certainly were no black men to date. So, I threw myself into my career. After about three years, I decided to move closer to Chicago, where I would meet more blacks.

My work as an intern led to full-time employment with Arthur Andersen, and in January 1983 I was made a Training Evaluation Specialist. During the next several years, I went through a series of promotions. In 1991, I was made a director and now supervise about forty-five people.

Arthur Andersen has about twenty-five to thirty directors in St. Charles. I am the only black and one of five women directors. The people within Arthur Andersen have been very supportive of me, and my career has progressed nicely. I certainly don't experience any blatant discrimination. At times, I theorize that clients don't take to me as well as they might to a white male. My work has gotten more difficult as I move up in the organization. The difficulty has less to do with my work talents than with my ability to socialize, to network. I think that if I were a white male it would be easier.

In 1992, I had my first real association with an openly gay man. He was a person on my staff. I didn't know him well, but when I heard he told his work group that he was gay, I decided to talk to him. I told him that I thought he was a brave man and I wanted him to know that I would be there to support him if he needed me. I knew it would be difficult for him. I guess because I felt different from most of the people around me, I could understand what he might be going through. I wanted him to know that he mattered to me and I wanted him to know that I would support him if anyone tried to discriminate against him. There seem to be little, if any, negative consequences. It just hasn't been an issue.

In 1990, I chaired the diversity committee of the National Society for Performance and Instruction (NSPI), my professional organization, and then served as a member of that committee. When we began that work, I thought of diversity in terms of race or culture. As time passed and I learned more about others, I expanded my thinking and now realize that diversity is far broader, including gays and lesbians, and people with other differences. I have been around a number of gays and lesbians in NSPI and can honestly say I am comfortable around all of them.

I think gays and lesbians have a tough life because they can't be themselves without being concerned for their own well-being. Even though they have some limited legal protections, gays and lesbians are not totally accepted. They can't walk down the street holding hands with the people they love and feel safe. I know they can't talk about their spouses, their lovers and be accepted and not have to worry about it. I think if there were an opportunity for straights to walk in a gay person's shoes, the world would be more tolerant of differences. Every day, I think about my color. I imagine homosexuals think every day about being a homosexual.

Last night I went to buy some gasoline. There was an Asian man at the station who spoke very broken English. The attendant asked him for his license number. The Asian wrote it down and handed it to him. When he left, the attendant said to me, "They have no business here in the United States. If they can't speak English, they don't belong here." I turned to him and said, "You know, we have to be more tolerant of people." I was very pleased with myself for not colluding with his prejudice. It really didn't matter whether he was Asian, black, gay, or whatever.

Recently, I spoke to a group of high school students in Anchorage, Alaska. One of them asked something like, "Do you ever wish you were different?" I told them I don't question who I am (I am an African American woman). I said I would probably have a different life if I were of another color, but I've had a wonderful life and every year gets better. I have a mission in life—to make sure other blacks make it. I don't quibble that I'm getting older either, or that I'm changing, or that I am getting gray hair. These experiences have all made me a stronger person. They have made me who I am today.

I learned about work from my father, but I learned about acceptance from my mother, a giving, kind woman. That's part of how I grew up. I have nothing to lose by accepting people as they are. They don't hurt me in any way. They don't take anything away from me. Being accepting makes life easier.

> Constance Holmes tells how her experiences of growing up in an all-black community have helped her become a champion of an all-inclusive workplace. Like Dale Barr, Constance became supportive as a result of interacting with a gay man at work and then, like Vince, integrated her experiences of prejudice with those of her gay coworker. As a result, she began to understand how important it is to support *all* workers. She experienced further insight and growth through her work as the chair of NSPI's Diversity Committee. By her active involvement, she realized that diversity was not just about race or culture but about inclusion of all people who are different, including sexual minorities. Her experience demonstrates that working to create an all-inclusive workforce provides opportunities and experiences that will increase one's confidence and competence.

Making It Work

Diversity in Action

5

We know that performance can be improved by clearly defining and communicating an organizational purpose and by detailing and aligning the organization's values, aims or goals, key jobs, objectives, and systems (financial, management, and so forth) behind the purpose or mission of the organization. We also know that bringing to life the organizational purpose is enhanced by ensuring that *all employees* have the knowledge and skills to perform as desired and that *all employees* see themselves included in this alignment.

If a performance system doesn't adequately exist, your organization will experience (unnecessary) performance problems. And, if employees (for whatever reason) do not consider themselves aligned with the organization, the likelihood of the organizational purpose coming to life is greatly diminished.

INCLUSION EQUALS PEFORMANCE

When it comes to issues around gays, lesbians, and bisexuals, these systems often fail because people lack the knowledge, skills, and resources to successfully execute them. They fail, too, because gays, lesbians, and bisexuals are excluded from the mix of employees and groups aligned behind organizational purposes. When people feel excluded, their commitment is usually less than when they feel included. That is no surprise. After all, how committed would you be to an organization that pretends you don't exist, or which purposely excludes you?

So, now you are going to look at actions you can take to make the workplace more inclusive. When it comes to taking action in this area, most managers don't know what to do. So, we've created a tool to help you translate your good intentions into good actions—actions that will equal better performance. It's called "101 Ways to Make Your Workplace More Inclusive." It's a tool we've designed and refined over the past several years. It includes a host of actions you can take. Some of these are simple and easy to implement immediately, like #8 which says, "Extend a welcome to newly hired sexual minorities," or #26, "Order and display gay publications like *10 Percent, Advocate, Out,* or *Victory.*" Other actions may be somewhat more complex and/or time consuming like #82: "Profile gays, lesbians, and bisexuals who embody your organizational values and those who make outstanding contributions within and outside of the company."

In using the list, take what you like and leave the rest. No one can apply all 101 actions described. But, everyone can apply many of them. The actions you take will help make the workplace more inclusive.

101 WAYS TO MAKE YOUR WORKPLACE MORE INCLUSIVE

1   Champion an all-inclusive organization.
2   Adopt a company-wide nondiscrimination policy that specifically includes sexual orientation.
3   Let the message ring loud and clear that you will not tolerate even subtle forms of discrimination.
4   Stand firm in the face of criticism and pressure.
5   Review personnel policies and procedures to remove any homophobic/heterosexist references.
6   Link being inclusive to being productive.
7   When interviewing candidates for jobs, let them know that your organization is all-inclusive.
8   Extend a big welcome to newly hired sexual minorities.
9   Add a domestic partnership option to the usual "married/single" choice.

101 Ways to Make Your Workplace More Inclusive

10 Think before raising an eyebrow over a named beneficiary or an honest medical history.

11 Attend/support attendance of others at professional conferences that deal with sexual orientation and workplace issues, like the "Out and Equal Conference," sponsored by NGLTF, or company conferences like AT&T's annual LEAGUE Conference.

12 Post a "safe place" magnet or "Do Ask! Do Tell!" sticker in a visible spot in your office to denote that this is a place one can freely talk about these issues. (A safe place magnet depicts a pink triangle in a green circle and can be purchased by contacting AT&T's LEAGUE, listed under resources in chapter 7.)

13 Promote, sanction, and even subsidize for all employees educational and training programs that promote better understanding and tolerance.

14 Encourage lesbian and gay employees to point out training and business policies and practices that discriminate based upon the sexual orientation of employees and customers.

15 Use examples of same-sex couples in business exercises, training role-plays and so forth.

16 Make gay and lesbian employees visible in your organization's newsletters and other communications.

17 Be sure to specifically invite same-sex partners to company events, travel, and so forth where spouses are traditionally included.

18 Especially welcome same-sex partners and guests at company events.

19 Recognize gays, lesbians, and bisexuals for their role in volunteer work.

20 If you have a company matching policy for charitable contributions, let it apply to any group with IRS 501 (c) 3 standing. In other words, enable employees to contribute to organizations that support sexual minorities. Your Human Resources or Personnel group knows how to do this.

21 Contribute money to gay groups or AIDS organizations in an employee's name.

22 Support and sponsor events that raise money for AIDS organizations.

23 Volunteer at a gay, lesbian, bisexual, or AIDS organization.

24 Gather together a group of employees to make a panel for the "NAMES Project" quilt in memory of employees who have died of AIDS. The quilt is a mosaic made up of homemade panels sewn by loved ones and friends of people who have died of AIDS.

25 Wear a "Straight But Not Narrow" button, available at most lesbian and gay bookstores.

26 Order and display gay publications, like *10 Percent*, the *Advocate*, *Out*, or *Victory* where other magazines are displayed.

27 Encourage gay, lesbian, and bisexual employees to form their own social and support groups.

28 Promote the use of e-mail to form gay, lesbian, and bisexual networks.

29 Bring gay, lesbian, and bisexual speakers into the workplace to talk about workplace and/or social issues. Chapter 7 identifies consultants and others who provide such services.

30 Attend gay social and support groups to demonstrate your support.

31 Celebrate diversity. Sponsor a potluck or other social event.

32 Promote gay-owned businesses. Ask employees for names of businesses and suppliers that are owned by sexual minorities.

33 Showcase positive images of gays, lesbians, and bisexuals.

34 Put the word out that if people have to "hide" who they are they will be wasting valuable corporate time and personal energy that could be well spent contributing to the profitability of the company.

35 Publicize upcoming gay-related events.

36 Use National Coming Out Day (October 11) to acknowledge the contributions of gays and lesbians in the workplace.

37 Subscribe to gay newspapers. Most cities have gay newspapers, like the *Native* in Manhattan or the *Bay Area Reporter* and *Sentinel* in San Francisco.

38 Seek out opportunities to learn from transgender people (those who have changed or are in the process of changing their gender).

39 Encourage your gay, lesbian, and bisexual employees to

march under your company banner in the local Gay Pride Day march.

40 Regardless of your sexual orientation, march with your lesbian, gay, and bisexual coworkers.

41 Publicize organizations like P-FLAG (Parents and Friends of Lesbians and Gays), which support people learning about gay and lesbian issues.

42 Encourage employees to take workshops and classes that educate around these issues.

43 Ask openly gay, lesbian, and bisexual employees about important community events, such as Gay Pride Day, National Coming Out Day, and so forth.

44 Note in your calendar National Coming Out Day (October 11), Gay Pride Day, and other dates important to gays, lesbians, and bisexuals.

45 On Gay Pride Day and National Coming Out Day fly the Rainbow Flag at work locations.

46 Respond to homophobic jokes and statements by saying, "That's not okay in this organization."

47 Review, on a regular basis, employees' responsibility to be nondiscriminatory.

48 Sponsor noontime forums to educate employees about gay and lesbian workplace issues.

49 Establish a gay, lesbian, and bisexual section in your corporate library.

50 Sponsor a booth at gay pride events and other important celebrations.

51 Route business and news articles about gay and lesbian workplace issues to people within your organization.

52 Provide feedback that reinforces and develops behaviors that contribute to making the workplace more inclusive.

53 Provide public as well as private recognition to employees who are contributing to making the workplace more inclusive.

54 Document evidence of supporting an all-inclusive workforce in employees' performance appraisals.

55 Give rewards (raises, promotions, time off) to employees who demonstrate making the workplace more inclusive.

56 Keep higher-ups informed about the contributions of gay, lesbian, and bisexual employees.

57 Avoid cliques established on the basis of sexual orientation.

58 Ask about a sick loved one.

59 Offer to lend a hand to gays and lesbians who take care of ill partners or friends.

60 Give your gay employees time off to attend funerals of close friends.

61 Ensure that gays and lesbians, are given bereavement leave when a same-sex partner passes away.

62 Take coffee or have meals with people who have a different sexual orientation than you.

63 Acknowledge and celebrate the commitment ceremonies of gays and lesbians.

64 Ask about the partners of your gay, lesbian, or bisexual co-workers.

65 Acknowledge and celebrate the birth or adoption of children of same-sex partners.

66 Let your gay, lesbian, and bisexual employees know that you will stand up for them in the event they experience any discrimination.

67 Encourage employees to bring harassment or discrimination complaints to you.

68 Refer employees experiencing harassment or discrimination to the proper authorities within the organization.

69 Follow up to ensure that harassment or discrimination cases are being vigorously and fairly pursued.

70 Recognize and acknowledge the creative perspective your gay, lesbian, and bisexual employees bring to the workplace.

71 When putting together information packets for conferences and out-of-town guests, include information on gay, lesbian, and bisexual places of interest (restaurants, social venues, and so on). Include a copy of your local gay paper.

72 When appropriate, encourage your gay, lesbian, and bisexual employees to recommend other sexual minorities for jobs within the organization.

73 DO NOT assume that employees (or customers) are heterosexual.

74 Let openly gay, lesbian, and bisexual employees know that you're happy they are "out."

75 Let employees know what they are expected to do regarding

workplace issues related to gays and lesbians (see chapters 3 and 5).

76 Advertise in the gay press and at gay events.

77 Share what other successful companies are doing in the area of gay, lesbian, and bisexual workplace issues.

78 Thank those of other sexual orientations for demonstrating their support for you.

79 Ask gay, lesbian, and bisexual employees to post notices of special importance.

80 Make a regular spot on your company bulletin board for information relevant to issues of sexual orientation and to announce important upcoming events.

81 Use your internal newsletters, magazines, and other publications to highlight sexual orientation issues and to recognize employees who have contributed to making the workplace more inclusive.

82 Profile gays, lesbians, and bisexuals who embody your organizational values and those who make outstanding contributions within and outside of the company.

83 Post a list of gay-related organizations that relate to the workplace.

84 Subscribe to organizations such as Overlooked Opinions, a national marketing research firm, that focus on the gay and lesbian market.

85 Take political action on gay and lesbian issues, such as writing letters or contacting political representatives, and let your co-workers know what action they can take.

86 Use the gay media and gay community organizations to specifically recruit gays, lesbians, and bisexuals.

87 Respond to criticism by referring to your desire to create and be part of an all-inclusive workplace.

88 Use the words gay, lesbian, and bisexual as part of your everyday vocabulary (you will become totally comfortable).

89 Keep higher-ups informed about the sizable lesbian, gay, and bisexual market.

90 Keep higher-ups informed about important issues and events related to sexual orientation.

91 Use the resources of the business and community organizations listed in chapter 7 to gain knowledge of these issues.

92 Support, where feasible, attendance at outside courses that relate to sexual orientation workplace issues.

93 Ask employees who attend these courses to tell others about their experiences.

94 Write letters of appreciation to employees who have contributed to making the workplace more inclusive.

95 Select openly gay, lesbian, and bisexual employees to represent the company/your organization at internal/external events.

96 Include openly gay, lesbian, and bisexual individuals on company boards and task forces.

97 Have fun around these issues, without putting anyone on the spot.

98 Smile when you say the words "gay," "lesbian," and "bisexual."

99 Do ask openly gay, lesbian, and bisexual people to tell you about their lives.

100 Do tell about your experiences as a sexual minority or supporter.

101 Let others know about *A Manager's Guide to Sexual Orientation in the Workplace* and purchase copies for those who you think would find it especially valuable!

No one person is expected to remember each of the 101 ways to make your workplace more inclusive. What is important about the list is the spirit behind it. In other words, there *are* many things people can do that would make others feel more included. And that's good business if you expect your employees to get behind your goals and your customers to buy your products. (By the way, this list can easily be modified to support any of the diverse groups of people who find themselves minorities in their organizations.)

A MODEL DIVERSITY POLICY

The National Society for Performance and Instruction (NSPI) is America's premiere professional organziation dedicated to improving human performance. With a membership of ten thousand chapter and international members, NSPI has developed a diversity policy that is a model for other organizations to follow because it is so all-inclusive. The policy, which can be easily adapted to fit your organization, is shown below.

NSPI Diversity Policy

NSPI is an all-inclusive Society. It values differences in people and diversity within our organization and our profession. It recognizes the different perspectives and contributions an all-inclusive people can make to improving human performance.

It is NSPI's policy to welcome and reach out to people of different ages, races, nationalities, ethnic groups, genders, physical abilities/qualities, sexual/affectional orientations, health status, recovery status, religions, backgrounds and educational experiences, incomes, material status, marital or parental status, class, military experiences, and geographic locations, as well as to any others, who may from time to time experience discrimination or abuse.

NSPI does not discriminate against any group or individual. In fact, the organization will actively oppose any and all forms of discrimination.

It is also NSPI's desire to help others (clients, customers, constitiuents, and colleagues) to develop similar policies and support diversity and performance improvement within the workplace.

NPSI's policy is important because it is so totally inclusive. Since NSPI introduced the policy, a core of leaders from the organization have worked hard to bring the policy to life. The result has been a visible increase in conference attendance of each of the populations identified in the policy, especially people of differing races, physical abilites, nationalities, and sexual orientations. And this increase has occured during the tough economic times of the past few years.

We hope you join the many companies that are moving ahead to make the workplace all-inclusive. We think you will be surprised at how little the cost and how big the gain, as evidenced by the next section.

EQUAL BENEFITS: NOT SO COSTLY AFTER ALL

There are a number of concerns and fears that you may have regarding the inclusion of gay and lesbian employees and their committed partners in company health and other benefits. The following list provides some facts about possible concerns. As you will see the actual costs of offering equal benefits have been well below what many people had anticipated. Thus, the perception of equity that is acquired as a result of offering such benefits appears to be well worth the effort. In addition to the information provided in this section, see also the "News Articles" section in the Resource Guide on equal benefits.

Concern # 1:

The inclusion of gay and lesbian couples and their partners and dependents in company benefits will greatly increase costs.

FACT:

In 1990, the City of Seattle began offering equal benefits to their gay and lesbian employees and their committed partners. At the time, their insurance company imposed a surcharge to cover what they anticipated would be additional expenses. After two years, the insurance company canceled the surcharge because no evidence of additional costs attributable to the new policy could be found. (Also, see the *New York Times* article on benefits dated June 13, 1993.)

Concern # 2:

Treating people with AIDS will bankrupt the company's health plan.

FACT:

It is estimated that the average cost of treating an individual with AIDS is less than $50,000 per year. The average cost of treating a premature baby is in excess of $300,000. According to a number of sources, the insurance industry's top two concerns are problematic neonatal care and dependent-adolescent accidents.

Concern # 3:

Relationships without marriage are unstable and transitory.

FACT:

The Northern California chapter of LEAGUE (Lesbian, Gay, Bisexual United Employees of AT&T) polled their membership in 1993 and found that the average length of a committed relationship among members is 8.3 years, with the longest relationship lasting 18 years. Their figures compare to a median of 7.1 years for legally sanctioned heterosexual marriages, of which nearly half end in divorce.

Concern # 4:

Only a few companies have implemented equal benefits, and doing so might cause fundamentalist groups to view the company as championing gay rights.

FACT:

Hundreds of employers, including Apple Computer, ASK Software, Borland International, Boston's Children's Hospital, Ben and Jerry's, Canadian Press/Broadcast News, HBO, Levi Strauss, Lotus Development Corp., MCA, The San Francisco Giants, Sun Microsystems, Viacom, and Silicon Graphics, have already successfully implemented equal benefits. These companies are working to champion diversity and not simply the rights of any particular group (as claimed by some fundamentalist groups).

Concern # 5:

There is no need for such benefits. Unmarried heterosexual couples and lesbian and gay couples do not have children and, therefore, do not need dependent care benefits.

FACT:

> The Northern California chapter of LEAGUE found that 25% of their membership have children for whom they have primary care living at home with them.

AVOIDING ALIENATION AND CONTROVERSY

We recently served as a reference for *New York Times* business writer Barbara Noble. In researching her story, "A Quiet Liberation for Gay and Lesbian Employees" (the *New York Times*, Sunday, June 13, 1993), she found that most American corporations wanted to "do right" by their gay and lesbian employees and customers, but simply didn't know how to go about "doing right" without stirring up unwanted controversy. After some thought, we've come to a few conclusions that should be helpful to you in eliminating or reducing alienation and controversy.

First, it's evident that most people (78 percent, according to a September 1992 *Newsweek* poll) believe that gays and lesbians should be given equal rights and opportunities in the workplace. Second, controversy need not be stirred up, as evidenced by the quiet manner in which New Jersey became the eighth state to enact a law providing some form of job protection to gays and lesbians. (Nine states currently provide protection. These include: Wisconsin, Massachusetts, Hawaii, Connecticut, Minnesota, California, New Jersey, Vermont, and Rhode Island.) Third, the way to successfully address gay, lesbian, and bisexual workplace issues and reduce or eliminate controversy at the same time is to create something bigger than any one group. In other words, create an all-inclusive organizational diversity policy at the highest levels (company-wide, if possible) that includes gays, lesbians, and bisexuals, as well as all other groups that experience discrimination in the workplace. The "NSPI Diversity Policy" you just reviewed is an excellent model of an all-inclusive policy. By creating an all-inclusive policy you form a strong basis for subsequent, affirming action.

So, let's look at the action required to "do right" by your gay, lesbian, and bisexual employees and customers. We think that by adhering to the following seven steps, not only will you avoid alienation and controversy, but you may actually gain in performance results. We also think you will cement the loyalty of your gay, lesbian, and bisexual employees and customers, and send a strong message that *everyone* is welcome within your organization and *no one* will be discriminated against. That kind of strong action will build commitment and loyalty!

Seven Steps to Avoiding Alienation and Controversy
(How to improve performance results and gain employee and customer loyalty and commitment.)

1   *Identify key influencers in your organization.*
    Key influencers are people, regardless of job or level, who are instrumental in influencing others. From this list identify where these influencers stand on development of an all-inclusive diversity policy.

>> Ask those who support it,
    "What would you be willing to do to help make such a policy a reality in the organization?"

>> Ask those who aren't sure where they stand on the issue,
    "What needs to take place for you to support development of such a policy?"

>> Ask those who are against it,
    "What needs to happen for you to move to be neutral or even positive about such a development?"

The answers you get will provide you with the information you need to move ahead.

2   *Develop an all-inclusive diversity policy.*
    Bring together representatives from every diverse population to develop this policy. Ask people to tell their stories about what it's like to be a woman, gay, Asian, disabled, over fifty, and so on. Use a competent facilitator to carry the group through this process.

    DO NOT EXCLUDE ANYONE!

3   *Garner support of your new policy from the rest of the organization.*
Have the representatives meet with people within each organization to gain buy-in. Have the representatives describe the experience they went through and detail the policy. Asking participants to chose the statement that best matches their feelings, use the following statements in an anonymous poll to identify participant "buy-in" to policy.

3 = "The policy is excellent. I see myself included."
2 = "The policy is good. I see myself included."
1 = "The policy is lousy. I don't see myself included."

Array the polling results and develop an average. For example, if five people rated the policy excellent, four good and one poor, you would record on an easel pad or whiteboard,

3 3 3 3 3 2 2 2 2 1

To find the average, simply add up all the numbers and divide by the number of people who participated. In the above example, the numbers added together equal 24. Divide 24 by 10 (the number of participants) and you arrive at an average of 2.4.

If the average is **2.0 or higher**, thank everyone for participating and let them know you will do your best to bring the policy to life within your organization.
If the average is **1.5 to 1.9**, collect ideas for improving the policy and review these with the original team of representatives.
If the average is **1.4 or less**, toss the policy and start the process over.

4   *Demonstrate high-level support for the policy.*
Do something that shows the policy has support at all levels within the organization. Use the list "101 Ways to Make Your Workplace More Inclusive" to help you identify appropriate actions.
5   *Stand firm in the face of criticism of your actions.*
Avoid being defensive or argumentative. When faced with

criticism, quietly refer to your organization's diversity policy and state that you are committed to bring that policy to life. Let the person know that if there is anyone in the organization who feels left out, including the person criticizing the policy, that you believe the performance of the organization will suffer. After all, how committed can anyone be to an organization that excludes them?

6   *Put the word out that you will tolerate no discrimination of any kind and back up those words with quick action at the slightest hint of discrimination.*
By taking quick action you reduce the likelihood of further workplace discrimination, and you may avoid costly legal battles.

7   *Embrace and celebrate the diversity within your organization.*
Today's workplace is a diverse one. You can fight this diversity or you can join the growing list of corporations that are embracing and celebrating it. Look for ways to embrace and celebrate the diversity within your organization. Link the celebrations to performance results, where possible. Organizations that embrace and celebrate diversity today are positioning themselves for a successful future, as the workforce becomes more and more diverse.

By making the workplace more inclusive, employers strengthen employee commitment to organizational goals, as well as employee and customer loyalty. According to a recent article in the *New York Times* (March 2, 1992, p. D9), gays and lesbians are very aware of which companies are reaching out to them. And that awareness will translate into increased or descreased performance and sales results. By adhering to the seven steps outlined above, we think you can make your organization all-inclusive without needlessly alienating others and creating controversy.

Deepening
Knowledge

6

Family, Friends, and
the Impact of Culture

We would now like to introduce you to three heterosexual family members—a father, a brother, and a mother—and to a gay man who describes the interplay of culture and family on his sexual orientation.

In the first story, Art Moreno tells of coming to accept and speak out in support of his gay son. His is the story of a man whose Hispanic culture and Catholic upbringing led him to feel, initially, as though he were being punished by having a gay son. Art describes how his connection to other parents (through an organization called P–FLAG—Parents and Friends of Lesbians and Gays) helped him to accept his son and how he became a champion for his son's right to be who he is. Next, Frank Wong tells of his birth in Vietnam, his growing up in Hong Kong and Canada, and his life in the U.S. Frank's story shows how dramatically a gay man's history can influence his life.

Mick Miller then tells of the challenges both he and his brother faced as children and how his brother's homosexuality *and* his illness brought them closer together and led Mick to discover his own humanity and connection to others. Mick's moving story will enable you to understand the potential impact illness of a loved one, coupled with issues of sexual orientation, have on the productivity of both heterosexual and gay employees and lays the foundation for you to learn new ways to offer support and help.

In the final story, Luann Conaty describes her life as a fundamentalist and her journey to accept her gay son. Her story illustrates the challenges that many heterosexuals are likely to experience upon learning of the homosexuality or bisexuality of a family member. In particular, her story, Art's, and Mick's, describe the "coming out" process that heterosexuals face when a relative or close friend comes out to them.

Managers who are aware of and sensitive to the coming out process of both homosexuals and heterosexuals are an excellent resource to all employees and colleagues, especially those who are either acknowledging their own sexual identity or that of a loved one. These stories provide insight and awareness to help you become that kind of manager.

Art Moreno

Small Business Owner

I was born on March 16, 1934, and experienced what I believe to have been a very normal childhood. I was the middle of five children. I had two older brothers and two younger sisters (one of whom died of a diabetes-related condition a few years back). My family was Catholic and I was raised with Catholic beliefs.

My father worked for a photographic services company in El Paso, Texas. Beginning in grammar school and throughout my schooling I spent evenings and Saturdays working with him. My father taught me in order to prepare me for a career. In high school, I worked in a photography studio and, although I was somewhat envious of my friends who did not have to work on Saturdays, I enjoyed the money. In addition, I learned a great deal from the owner of the studio. He had worked in the carnival and really knew how to "work" people, how to promote himself. It was a fascinating education. I was the school photographer at my high school and I won awards for my photography.

In the (Catholic) environment in which I was raised, sex was never discussed at home. So, homosexuality was never mentioned. Sex was something I learned about through my friends and life experiences. At the time, all I knew about homosexuality was that it was a sin and was wrong.

Homosexuality simply didn't concern me. My only contact with homosexuality was through movies. Whenever my friends and I saw obviously gay people in the movies we would make negative comments between ourselves. We never made such comments directly toward an actual gay person because we didn't have the chance—we didn't know any.

During my teenage years and my early twenties, I subscribed to the notion that homosexuals were bad. I don't know why, really. Certainly I was not that great. I mean, I had many flaws, being something of a womanizer and a partier. At the time, I thought the worst thing a father could have happen to him was to have a homosexual son. There was no logic or reason for believing this but I just felt that way. I felt that if God ever wanted to punish someone, that would be the way he would do it.

Well, God punished me (although he really blessed me) by giving me a son who is gay. Mark Steven is my fourth son, and when I first found out he was gay, I was devastated. Once I found out, I planned to disown him unless he sought help and found a woman to marry so he could be in a heterosexual relationship.

I felt shame, guilt, and concern about what my friends and others would think. I was determined to get help for my son. I was very hurt. But, I see that I hurt him more by the lack of acceptance and the rigid stance I took. My relationship with Mark was strained. I couldn't deal with it, much less accept it, and I told him so. I was so unaccepting that he moved to Phoenix, where two of his brothers lived. In the midst of all this, I met an openly gay, celibate Catholic priest, who I hired to work for me while he was on sabbatical.

If it wasn't for this priest's help and my three older sons, who were very accepting of Mark—and for that I am now very grateful—I don't know if I would have been able to get to the point where I am now. The priest told me about Parents and Friends of Lesbians and Gays, commonly known as P-FLAG. I began to attend meetings, and they were very revealing and very rewarding. The meetings offered me the chance to share my pent-up feelings and let me know that there are a lot of parents in varying stages of acceptance when it comes to their gay children.

As time went by, I continued to attend P-FLAG meetings. I read all that I could get my hands on and I came to realize that homosexuality is not a choice and that only God knows why some people turn out to be gay. Soon, communications with my son increased and our relationship and love blossomed. I no longer think of Mark as my homosexual son but as a warm, loving, friendly, thoughtful, considerate creature of God, who now knows my heart. I became accepting of my son.

Time passed. Soon Mark brought his lover home for Christmas. I knew his cousins (my nephews) whom he grew up with would be at the house and I wasn't sure if they knew if he was gay or not. So, I got them all together before Mark arrived to let them know that he was gay. I simply wanted to prepare them in the event that they did not know and that he would be coming with his lover. I also wanted to see if there would be any negative reactions. Their response floored me. They said, "So, what's the big deal? He's our cousin and we love him." That was the extent of it.

I became very active in P-FLAG. One day, one of our local county commissioners made a very disgusting comment publicly that to contain AIDS all homosexuals should be castrated. Until then, I had been closeted about my son's homosexuality. Only family members and friends who needed to know were told my son is gay. "I didn't make an issue of his sexuality," I thought. I was simply trying to deal with it, understand it and accept it. But, when the county commissioner spoke so ignorantly, so hatefully, I just didn't feel right in doing nothing about it. I spoke with my wife and all of my sons and told them that I planned to go public and stand up for what I believed was right and, perhaps, to try to make up to my gay son for all the hurt that I caused him as well as to stand and speak as a heterosexual to defend the gay community.

I was given one hundred percent support from my sons and wife. This was a big step for me to take—to go public and come out of the closet about my son. I just knew in my heart that I had to do it.

I told a priest friend of mine (not the one mentioned earlier) that I was planning to go to commissioners' court and make a statement admonishing the commissioner. My friend, the priest, accompanied me. This is the essence of the statement I made:

> *I am here to address the AIDS issue and to respond to Mr. Fonseca's recent statement. I come first as a concerned father of a gay son who resides out of El Paso and whom I love very much.... I represent P-FLAG, a support group of parents and friends of lesbians and gays, and on their behalf I wish to respond to the recent insensitive and bigoted remarks made by Commissioner Fonseca concerning AIDS and the gay community.*
>
> *It is particularly distressing to witness an elected official display in public such ignorance and prejudice about a subject so serious. His attempt to explain away his intolerant comments by saying he was only making a joke shows not only bad judgment, but callous disrespect for us all. In addition, to try to explain his prejudice by referring to his religious beliefs is equally deploring. All the religions we know teach understanding and compassion not ridicule and intolerance.*
>
> *If Mr. Fonseca is truly concerned about AIDS in our city and the potential high cost of care for those afflicted with this dreaded virus, then we suggest he spearhead a concerted city-county effort to provide the necessary funds to educate our community about the virus and how it can be avoided— because the affected population is everywhere. Every dollar spent now for such education will surely save hundreds, maybe thousands of dollars later.*
>
> *We ask all locally elected officials to fully inform themselves about this serious problem and take a leadership role in*

helping to solve it rather than stooping to, as Mr. Fonseca has, making unproductive crude comments in public which vilify those unfortunate persons afflicted by the virus.

Mr. Fonseca has embarrassed all fair-minded El Pascans by his recent actions. We can only hope the voters in his district remember this embarrassment when they next have the opportunity to vote.

My comments made the television news and, surprisingly, of some twenty-five or thirty telephone calls and comments made by customers and friends coming into my photography store, all but one came to express their support for me and my position. The one that didn't was a little old lady who wanted to read scripture to me. It was a great feeling to know that I had done the right thing and I was reassured by the positive comments that were made.

My wife and I remain actively involved in P-FLAG, helping parents to understand and love their children, and we are also involved with the Southwestern AIDS Committee as advocates. I have been blessed and fortunate to be the advocate for two young men, one heterosexual and one homosexual, who have since passed away from AIDS. Both were very angry young men when I began as their advocate but as time passed our bonding and friendship grew. I feel that I was instrumental in helping each to reestablish a relationship with God.

As St. Francis of Assisi said:

Oh Divine Master grant that I may not so much seek to be consoled as to console. To be understood as to understand. To be loved as to love. For it is in giving that we receive.

I am blessed with a gay son without whom these wonderful life experiences would never have been possible.

Art's cultural and religious background led him initially to feel that having a gay son was punishment from God. But as you read, he moved through his early shame to actively supporting his son and the gay community. Art's story demonstrates the positive impact of finding support from other parents. It is critical that managers find support from other managers to effectively deal with sexual orientation issues. Putting into practice the skills in this book should help you to develop relationships in your effort to create a better workplace.

Frank Y. Wong

Psychologist

Homosexuality is recorded in Chinese civilization and reached a peak during the Sung Dynasty (circa 1000 A.D.) Many gays during this dynasty gave Chinese civilization some of its greatest literature. For the most part, the various forms of Buddhism and Taoism do not see homosexuality as a sin. In fact, in Mahayana Buddhism, being gay is due to one's karma. Today, however, most Chinese think that gays are abnormal. They generally tolerate homosexual acts so long as men "procreate" and keep their homosexuality to themselves.

My name is Frank. I am a Chinese-American, born in Vietnam (formerly South Vietnam). My parents, ethnic Chinese, were born in China. They and their parents moved to Vietnam after the Chinese Communist Government took power in the Motherland in the late 1940s.

Even for people who are familiar with Chinese cultural practices, some explanation is usually required to understand my family background. My father, the youngest of five children, came from a very wealthy family. Following Chinese tradition, my paternal grandparents arranged for my father, at age sixteen, to marry one of his first cousins, a daughter of his aunt. One is allowed to marry a first cousin as long as she or he is from the maternal aunt's side (a tradition based on no scientific evidence). The woman my father married at sixteen is not my biological mother but according to custom, I call her "Mother." Their union resulted in nine children. Like other ancient cultures (such as Indian and Arabic), Chinese culture allowed male polygamous marriages. Although this practice is no longer legal in China, it was common among my father's family and other wealthy families when he was young. Thus, when my father was about thirty years old, he met another woman roughly his age whom he married and with whom he eventually had two more sons and a daughter. I was the second son and the middle child of this subset of the family. According to the same custom, I call my biological mother "Aunt." Although my father was well versed in traditional Chinese culture, I sense that he met and "fell in love" with Aunt (my biological mother) in an almost Western way. Educated by the French, he raised us in a less-than-orthodox Chinese fashion.

Fortunately my two mothers got along well with each other. I attribute the harmonious relationship between them to the fact that my father maintained two households and that both my mothers are faithful Mahayana Buddhists. Mahayana Buddhists believe that Buddha is God, while Hinayana Buddhism (the original belief), which I practice, honors Buddha as a mortal human being.

My father was not very religious, nor were most of my extended family (aunts, uncles, cousins), which is atypical of most Chinese.

Communication in my family was very complex. At home I usually conversed with my father and "Aunt" and, sometimes, my "mother" in Cantonese. With my paternal grandfather, my father's brothers, and other extended family members, I spoke Chiu-Chownese. "Aunt" had to learn to speak Chiu-Chownese when she married my father. My father and I also, occasionally, spoke in Mandarin and French. I attended a multilingual, Catholic school in Vietnam, and classes were taught in Vietnamese, Mandarin, and French.

Growing up in my family was not easy. Because of our lineage and social status in South Vietnamese society (we were a prominent business family), I realized, even as a young child, that we were somewhat different from others. Lineage and customs are so important in Chinese families that a different name is given to designate similar kinships (e.g., cousin from the mother's side versus cousin from the father's side). My father's first name indicates his position within a span of twelve generations in the extended family.

Looking back, I suspect that my parents were often torn between the demands imposed by Chinese tradition and their Westernized experiences. My father gave some of us Christian first names and Chinese middle names. Life was also complicated by the visibility my father experienced as a highly successful businessman. He was repeatedly asked by the president of South Vietnam to become a naturalized citizen. He compromised by changing his Chinese name to a Vietnamese-sounding name while remaining a legal alien. We, his children, were Vietnamese citizens. Like my father, I have often felt torn between the push and pull of differing expectations.

In Chinese families, emotion is seldom expressed or talked about. Yet my father openly showed affection for "Aunt," though not for "Mother." He also showed affection for his daughters and his youngest sons, including me. Yet my three older brothers, expected to adhere to strict roles, were shown no affection whatsoever.

I spent summers with my "mother" and the rest of the year with "Aunt." When I was about five years of age, I had my first sexual experience with one of my half brothers. He was a year older than me. I recall it as an enjoyable and pleasant experience and one to which I attributed little thought or significance. I think my parents were aware of the incident—they probably thought it was just child's play—although they chose to say nothing about it. My brother and I continued to "play" for about two months until I returned to my "Aunt's" house.

Upon my return from the summer of my first sexual experience, I had several encounters with one of my father's gardeners. He was seventeen, a pleasant, well-built fellow, who initiated these encounters (by today's standards, he might be accused of sexually abusing me). Like many Chinese, the gardener found a girlfriend once our encounters ended. I recall these experiences as enjoyable, pleasant.

About this time, my parents decided to move our immediate family to Hong Kong. They had lost all confidence in the South Vietnamese government and selected Hong Kong because our extended family already had businesses there. Although a British crowned colony, Hong Kong was predominantly a Chinese society with few political overtones (or at least, that was the case in the early 60s). So, in 1965, at the age of six, I went to Hong Kong. Eventually, my father's side of our extended family joined us. The family's business headquarters were relocated there as well.

The move was exciting—Hong Kong was a very modern society—and it was difficult. While I spoke Mandarin, French, and Vietnamese, I did not speak English, which was the official language of Hong Kong (it is now bilingual). I also found it difficult to live in an apartment, after being raised in the large open spaces of South Vietnam. And, I missed my friends and the relatives who stayed behind. To overcome my anxieties, I channeled all my energy into school.

I attended a private bilingual school. I was a straight-A student, yet bored by the curriculum that emphasized rote memorization. To fill my time, I read incessantly. When I was thirteen and fed up with traditional schooling, I pleaded with my parents to let me transfer to a more innovative international school. After much persuasion and many antics on my part, they agreed. In my new school, I learned how to think as an individual. It was a rich experience—a classic case of "East meets West"—and I grew as a result of wrestling with such conflicts. I also began to play competitive badminton, I took up swimming, and I began to travel the world, which my parents generously supported.

I loved my newfound independence. I maintained a straight-A record, but unlike most Chinese teenagers, I did things just to annoy my parents. I was becoming quite "westernized," and my parents became increasingly worried about my behavior. At a loss as to how to deal with me, they decided to send me to live with my older sister and two brothers, who now resided in Canada. They hoped that my older siblings would know how to deal with me. I welcomed the opportunity and left for Toronto in 1975 at the age of sixteen. (I later learned that my parents were also preparing me for the future, as they thought that eventually Hong Kong would return to China, as it will in 1997.)

In Toronto, I attended a private Catholic high school. My parents hoped that upon graduation I would attend the University of Toronto, one of Canada's most prestigious universities. My father and "Aunt" also wanted me to major in business or "something useful"—meaning financially profitable. "Mother," however, simply wanted me to be happy in whatever I did and hoped that I would be spiritual.

I opted for the University of Guelph, a medium-sized university fifty-five miles west of Toronto, where my parents now lived. The distance enabled me to live apart from my folks, who by now thought of me as "unusual." "He's not your typical Chinese," they would say.

Once on my own, I developed a thirst to learn more about Chinese civilization. I became vice-president of the Chinese Student Association and was active in many campus activities, including varsity badminton. I majored in philosophy, which disappointed my father and "Aunt."

I began to seriously date a Chinese girl whom I had met during my last year in high school. My parents seemed pleased. While we liked each other a great deal, our relationship ended when she moved to Vancouver. I still had not come to terms with being gay.

When I was a senior in college, my father developed lung cancer. He was a very stubborn man and refused many major forms of treatment. He remained ill while I finished college and got my first job, as a mental health counselor, in Rochester, New York. He died on November 16, 1982.

I went to Hong Kong for the funeral. His death brought about many squabbles in our extended family, especially in regards to the family business. According to Chinese tradition, the last male in the patriarchal family becomes head of the extended family and controls the family businesses. Thus, one of my uncles took over, creating a family uproar that would rival any seen on the TV programs *Dynasty* or *Dallas*. As a result, our family name was constantly in the media. And there was litigation, which took nine years to resolve. As faithful Mahayana Buddhists, "Mother" and "Aunt" did not intervene in these squabbles, and in the end my immediate family lost almost everything—money and lineage. My three older brothers, who had seen it as their duty to protect and maintain the family name, felt great shame. My greedy uncle disgraced six generations of the family name.

Like "Mother" and "Aunt," I stayed out of the squabbles—a stand not very popular among some of my siblings. Yet I was determined to maintain some sense of myself, not wanting these squabbles to draw me back into the family whirlpool. Nevertheless, I became quite depressed about my father's death. He and I had a lot of unfinished personal business and I wish that I had been able to tell him who I really was, despite how difficult that would have been given our cultural heritage.

Following my father's death, I met several individuals who significantly affected my life. I found myself attracted to an older man. I was taken by his blond hair and blue eyes and flattered that he was taken by me. For the first time in my life, I fell in love, and we began what turned out to be a very short-lived relationship. There were troubling signs from the very beginning. Claiming to be an heir to the Upjohn Pharmaceutical Company fortunes, he was constantly broke and, like a fool, I constantly gave him whatever money he needed. I soon discovered that he was lying about a number of things, including an affair he was having with someone else. That was all I could handle and I ended the relationship, which cost me so, both emotionally and financially.

I was hurt and lonely. Shortly afterwards, I met a Hungarian-American woman. She was six years my senior. I also met a man who was ten years older than I. I dated both of them simultaneously and told each of them about the other. Neither seemed to mind. They turned out to be my best friends, accepting me completely—the good and the bad parts—and treating me like an individual. They keenly understood how conflicted I was by the demands imposed by eastern and western cultures. Their advice to me was always "to be myself."

Because of these two dear friends, I realized that I needed to work on some of my personal issues. I started seeing a therapist. Therapy helped me to come to terms with many of these conflicts and address the relevant issues surrounding my homosexuality and my family.

Given what I learned about homosexuality and Chinese civilization, I concluded that most of my family would allow me to quietly do my gay thing as long as I married and had children, but my experiences and therapy taught me to be true to myself. I simply wasn't prepared to lead a double life. I tried to communicate some of my feelings to my immediate family, but most of them preferred not to know. As a result, my relationship with my family has been strained. There were two exceptions, however. My two youngest sisters understood completely and, to this day, have been very supportive of me. Despite this strain posed by my family, I felt rejuvenated by my therapy and plotted a new course for my life.

I went to graduate school at Texas A&M University, where I attained a Ph.D. in social psychology. Both the majority of my fellow graduate students and faculty were supportive of my being openly gay. Following university, I joined the staff of Hofstra University, in Long Island, New York, where I currently live as an openly gay man.

I have lived in the United States for twelve years now. My relationships with my family are slowing improving. While most of them still prefer not to hear about my being gay and I respect that, if the subject comes up I do not budge. I am being myself today.

In addition to dealing with my homosexuality, as a Chinese man I have also had to deal with racism. At times, it seems that being Chinese has often been more difficult than being gay. I have had little problem with being an openly gay psychologist or in other work settings. More difficult perhaps, is having to deal with others who assume that simply because I am gay or because I am Chinese, I know everything there is to know about being gay or Chinese. I don't. But I do know that being gay is a part of the whole of me, an important part. I would like to think that being gay is just another adventure in life.

Frank's story demonstrates the role that culture can play in dealing with issues of sexual orientation. His and his family's efforts to integrate Eastern and Western cultures show the conflicts that those from different backgrounds often experience. Add to these differences how each culture treats homosexuality and you can see the challenges that sexual minorities often face. Frank often had less difficulty integrating his sexuality into his work than his cultural background. This points out the importance of supporting an *all-inclusive* workplace rather than attempting to support some categories of difference while ignoring others. Most of us can either relate or understand that integrating multiple identities requires considerable effort and energy and a workplace that facilitates integration through inclusion is one that supports greater productivity and commitment to organizational goals and objectives.

Restaurant Owner

My name is Mick Miller, and I am a forty-one-year-old, white, heterosexual male. My story involves my early experiences and attitudes with homosexuality, people I have known, my own growth, sexuality (both heterosexual and homosexual), and the evolution of my values and beliefs.

My upbringing is important to my story. I've lived all my life in a rural area of New Jersey. I am the second son of Catholic parents, lower-middle class. I have three brothers, one older, two younger, and one younger sister. My mother died when I had just turned fourteen. My father died when l was twenty-seven. I also had another younger brother. He died two years ago, six days after his thirty-second birthday. The cause of his death was starvation. My family has a long history of alcoholism. My father was alcoholic, my mother co-alcoholic. I can't speak for my siblings, but I am an alcoholic in recovery as is my youngest brother. Our heritage is Irish-German.

Ours was a family that had strict unwritten rules: don't talk, don't trust, don't feel. We were expected to obey blindly, have unwavering loyalty, not question the authority of our elders, rise above the standard of living my parents had, and never make mistakes. We never said, "I love you." There was no need to—it was simply understood. When we were punished we were told, "This hurts us more than it hurts you. We're only doing it because we love you." That was when we were told we were loved. Irish-German Catholics: stiff, authoritative, fearful of the wrath of God—unless you were drunk, then you might loosen up a bit.

As a child I was not very happy. There were fun days and events, but basically I was miserable. I had to follow my older brother's footsteps and he had big feet and a long stride. I never lived up to my parents' expectations. I was told that anything I wanted to do was foolish, that I was a dreamer and dreamers never make it. My attainment of puberty and years of sexuality were fairly typical. I had crushes on girls since early childhood. I modeled myself after what I saw in the world around me. Mom and dad, lovers in movies and on TV, everything was heterosexual.

My first awareness of homosexuality came in the seventh grade. A friend of mine would come from school and pretend he was gay. What fun we had swishing, lisping, holding our wrists limp. He told me that was how queers acted. I had no idea what homosexuality was, but I thought I was learning all about "them."

I had a negative experience a few years later. Living in a rural community, it was common practice to hitchhike. School was fifteen miles away, and if you missed the bus home, you would simply thumb a ride. The fears of today were just not prevalent twenty-five years ago. Crime was virtually nonexistent in our area. One day I had to hitch a ride home, something I had done many times. Within five minutes I had a ride. The driver told me he had to stop at his house to let the dogs out. It sounded okay to me. His house was many miles away in territory I was not familiar with. He let the dogs out and asked if I would like to come in his house for a soda. I agreed. While in the house he took out some pornography and asked me if I had ever slept with a woman. I told him no. He came up in back of me, reached around me, and started to rub me. He asked me if I had ever had sex with a man and told me that he would, if I wanted him to. I pushed him away and said, "No." I told him that he had better take me home right away. On the way to my house he told me not to tell anyone what had happened. He said he meant no harm, that he would like to be friends. I was paralyzed with fear.

After he dropped me off I realized that he knew where I lived. I was terrified he would come back. That night I lay in my bed unable to sleep, just knowing he was coming back to get me. I woke my father and told him what had happened. The end result was that the police were contacted, and I showed them where the man lived. They arrested him and charged him with impairing the morals of a minor. He pleaded guilty and I have no idea what happened to him after that. I definitely had some strong feelings about "queers" by now. But it was more fear than hate. I'm sure that if I hadn't had future contact with homosexuals, my fears could have developed into the homophobic hate that is so prevalent in our society today.

At age eighteen I was working in a restaurant in a nearby town that had a large homosexual population. Many of the waiters and clients were gay. I was intrigued by them. They would act very campy in the kitchen, calling each other "Mary" and referring to a he as a she. It reminded me of what my friend had taught me back in the seventh grade. The hitchhike driver was a child molester. These men were not. At first I was fearful, but no one ever approached me. Eventually, feeling safer with them, I began to trust them. To me they were just a bunch of wild guys who loved to swish and lisp. I came to love being with them. They were clever and funny, qualities I admired.

Doug, a cook there, was about ten years my senior. He was a large man, about six-foot-three and 290 pounds. In his youth he was much slimmer and had worked as a female impersonator. In his later years he did parodies, Ethel Merman and the like. We became close friends. I would go to his house for dinner and got to know his parents quite well (they were aware of his sexual orientation). I felt at ease with him. He would take me to gay clubs and cabarets to see the impersonators and would introduce me to all the stars. Different jobs separated us and we lost touch with each other. I would occasionally talk to someone who had seen him and they would tell me how he was doing. About six years ago I read in the paper that he was murdered. I was deeply saddened. Doug had helped turn my fears into acceptance. He was someone who lived life as I did, but was sexually attracted to people of the same sex. Nothing more, nothing less. He influenced my beliefs and attitudes, and for that I will always be grateful. But the true test was yet to come.

My brother, Thom, would help me grow in ways I never dreamed possible. Thom was the "oddball" of the family. At birth, he had blond hair. No one in the family had blond hair. He was always frail as a child and even my youngest brother, one year younger than Thom, soon assumed a higher position in the pecking order. We used to tease Thom unmercifully as siblings do, since he was the weakest. He was Mom's pet. "Midgeon," she used to call him as an infant, combination of midget and pigeon, because he was so small and would make little cooing noises.

Thom excelled in school. He was a veritable genius and popular with everyone. He had poor athletic skills, which irked my father. Thom developed his artistic abilities by going into theater. I admired Thom for this because I also was not up to snuff in the athletic field, at least by my father's standards. I quit the basketball team in my junior year in order to be in the class play. What disappointments we were! My other brothers were wrestling stars (one a state champion), a basketball star, and a track star (with school records). Thom and I were nothings. Actors. Actors were dreamers. Actors were sissies, not "real men." So I could identify with Thom.

In our later years I pursued cooking (I was the only male in my home economics class) and photography, while Thom remained in theater. To our family, these were definitely artistic professions, and being artistic was equal to being unmanly. Thom's slight build, sensitivity, and lack of athletic demeanor made it even harder for him to break out of the family mold, but break out he did. For years I suspected Thom was gay. For years he didn't tell me. I was aware of the homosexual stereotype, and I observed that Thom had many girlfriends, but knew none that was steady. Actually, it was more of a gut feeling than a stereotype that made me wonder about Thom's sexual orientation.

About five years ago Thom "came out of the closet" to me. We talked about what it was like for him to grow up being gay, how tortured he felt by Dad. He didn't remember Mom well, as she died when he was still very young. Had I still been homophobic, I might have rejected Thom as our father did. I am grateful I didn't reject him. I believe we helped each other reach out for intimacy in a way neither of us had ever experienced. That leap of faith has helped me a great deal as I continue to strive for trust and meaning in close relationships.

In one of our conversations I asked if he was practicing safe sex. He said he was, but sex was not all that frequent. He simply could not find a lover. He had never been in a relationship. Any lover he ever did have had been casual or just someone he met in a club. Six months later, Thom came down with a cold that lingered on and on. When he finally went to a doctor, he was told it developed into pneumonia. Upon hospitalization, it was discovered he had AIDS. He said he probably contracted it about seven years earlier while in college. He had no idea who gave it to him, or who he may have given it to. All this happened during the time AIDS was new and not much was known about its transmission.

I was devastated by the news, but what shocked me most was my first reaction, anger. My first thought was "that's what you get for being queer." I was disappointed and surprised at myself. I thought I was beyond an attitude like that, but there it was— a value judgment directed at my brother. It only lasted a few seconds. I truly do not know if it was just a defense mechanism because my brother had just told me he was going to die soon, or if I still had, or have, prejudices against homosexuals. I want to believe the former.

During the next two years, Thom kept having bouts of pneumonia, each one lasting longer and weakening him further. For all the years he spent in the theater, he was never financially successful. He lived hand-to-mouth. The year before his diagnosis he finally quit the circuit and accepted a job as Assistant Professor of Theater Arts at a small university. He was finally earning a decent wage. After he learned he had AIDS, he quit his job and formed another theater company. He wanted to spend his remaining time doing the things he truly loved, even if it meant living hand-to-mouth again. He decided he wasn't dying with AIDS, but rather, he was going to live with AIDS.

He moved to Seattle, Washington, formed another company, and applied for and received grants to produce plays to be performed in the rural interior of the state for a summer cultural program. He was truly living. He even met a lover and had his first committed relationship. Just as the troupe hit the road for its first performance, Thom's lungs collapsed. He was driven 250 miles back to Seattle to be admitted to the hospital again. I received a call from my youngest brother, who lived in Baton Rouge. He said he was going to move to Seattle, to take care of Thom. He did and he ended up marrying a woman who was Thom's close friend.

A month later, Thom was back in the hospital. His lungs would not stay inflated. The doctors told him that they could operate by literally removing his lungs and abrading the outside to build scar tissue. The hope was that it would keep the air from escaping. He agreed to the operation. I called to talk to him the morning of the operation. I told him that I loved him very much and that if he died during the operation, that I would miss him very much. It was very hard for me to tell him that, but I didn't want him to die without having said how I felt. Remember that love was not spoken about in our house, it was assumed. God, how we needed to hear the words. Thom told me he loved me too and would wait for me if he died. I got a call later that night that he survived, but was in guarded condition. He was released several weeks later.

Upon returning home with my youngest brother, Thom's

health deteriorated rapidly. He was so weak and short of breath he could barely walk. He was admitted to the hospital again within a few weeks, this time fighting respiratory infections. It was at that point Thom decided to refuse any more treatment. He no longer wished to fight the inevitable. It was October when he told me about his decision. I flew out to see him one last time. When I got there he was emaciated, but in good spirits. He was refusing food and medication, all he had was saline drip and morphine for the pain.

We spent the week talking. I had remembered in therapy about my abuse and came to understand my sexual dysfunctions. I could identify with him all too well. Mom tortured me. Dad tortured him. We had both suffered shame and humiliation that affected our sexuality. I had trouble in relationships with women, he had trouble in relationships with men. We both had trouble dealing with intimacy and sexuality. We established a bond, a deeper understanding of ourselves and each other. He told me how he never felt "right." He always wanted to come out, but was afraid. He told me he so desperately wanted to be loved by our father, to be able to say "Dad, I'm gay, I'm everything you find repugnant, but I'm still your son. Can you tell me you love me? Can you love me for who I am unconditionally, not for what I do or what I don't do?" I found I could identify with his longing to be loved for who he was regardless of whether his lifestyle was acceptable to society or any individual.

I went home and called frequently. As the weeks passed he grew weaker and weaker. We began to use humor to lighten our moods. I would call and announce that I was "just seeing if you've died." He would respond, "not yet, but I'll call you as soon as I do." I told him I had an airplane reservation to come out during the Christmas season and asked if he thought he would live until then. He said he didn't think so. As the time grew near, I urged him to hold on until I got there so I could see him in person one last time. It was out of his hands now, he said, just as he always believed it had been.

He lived until I was able to get there during the holidays. On December 21, 1990, he celebrated his thirty-second birthday. He was not to have another. In the two months that had passed since I had seen him last, he had not eaten enough to keep a mouse alive. He looked like a person I had seen in a photo from the concentration camps in Nazi Germany. And yet he was full of life and spirit. We talked about spiritual things. About dying in peace. We talked so there would be no regrets. I said things to him so that after he died I would not be plagued by the thought, "I wish I had told him that before he died." I told him, again, how much I loved him and would miss him. He told me, again, that he would wait for me, that we would see each other again. It was a beautiful thought to me that the God we were taught to fear was going to accept us both. We both truly believed that the God who created us would not refuse our love. The God of our youth, we felt, had prejudiced men write the rules by which we were expected to abide. Our new God loves us just as we are, for we are only men and suffer the frailties of being human.

Every day when I left the hospital, I would kiss Thom good-bye. I was no longer ashamed. I had not kissed another man since I was a child. I stopped the day I decided I was too old to kiss my father. I was not afraid to catch AIDS, I was not afraid of what others might think. To love is to give and to give is to be humble. In our society I think there is nothing as threatening or possibly humiliating for most heterosexual men as kissing another man. Most would die first.

I left Seattle on December 26, 1990. When I left the hospital room that day I kissed Thom one last time. I knew I would never see him again in this life. It was so hard. We both knew it was the end. In the hallway I saw one of Thom's friends. I embraced him and I cried. He held me and cried, too. Two men, one gay, one straight, suffering the loss of another human being, found comfort and strength in each other that morning.

In our society Thom would not be accepted by the majority because he was gay. But to me he was one of the bravest, strongest men I have ever known. He overcame his fears, and accepted himself for who he was, unconditionally. He gave his love freely to all regardless of sexual orientation, sex, race, age, or any other characteristic that our society uses to differentiate us and assign value and judgment.

Two days after I left, Bob, the man by whom I was comforted

in the hospital, called to tell me Thom had died. He had taken his last curtain call.

Looking back I find it symbolic that Thom, who had been starved of love all his life, died of physical starvation. In the end he finally found the love he had longed for all his life. He loved himself, and many others loved him, too, unconditionally, and they told him so. He died a peaceful man.

I am now working on that same task. I am trying to truly love myself. I know what they mean now, when they say you need to love yourself before you can truly love another. There were many things I was taught as a child that I am now trying to unlearn. I recognize today, that it is important to respect all people, regardless of how different they are from me. I believe that people are like snowflakes, unique in their own right, and created by a loving God. I want to love unconditionally, the way Thom did. Since I can't change society, I am learning to act out my beliefs about the beauty of diversity with my many friends and acquaintances. As a restaurant owner, I have employed gays and lesbians. I find that my attitude towards them is a model for my employees. My concern is that they do the work I've hired them to do, just like everyone else. I seek out people who are loving and caring, regardless of their sexual orientation. As a result, I have made friends with exceptional people, gay and straight.

I still struggle with the prejudices I learned growing up. Today, I try to be aware of them, and challenge myself to change my thinking. I am finding that I have become intolerant of bigoted, small-minded people. Once an employee made a comment about "niggers." I told him to keep his thoughts to himself if he wanted to keep his job. Last year I saw an offensive bumper sticker on a motorcycle that was owned by an acquaintance. It said "AIDS CURES FAGS." I was furious. I fantasized about ways to hurt him. It is as if my prejudice now is about people who are prejudiced.

Even though my goal is acceptance of others unconditionally, I am afraid of not being accepted myself. I still have fears. I know what I am sexually and yet I would, at times, be very frightened to display any type of affection or behavior that might label me as homosexual. Still, there is a lot of hatred and fear in our society and, at times, I am not sure I want to put myself in a position that could threaten my life. It's as if I live in a paradox of fear that I'll be seen as less than a "real" man, and yet a real man would be sure enough of himself to express how he feels. I admire those who do have that courage. I am sure enough of myself, though, to write this story.

I am grateful that I am still alive and growing as a human being. I believe that children are not born homophobic, or with any other prejudice. Those traits are taught and can be unlearned if one's desire is strong enough. I have that desire. Just as I have had to unlearn my lessons about homosexuality, I have to continue to unlearn my lessons about my other prejudices. For those are the lessons that, in my opinion, are the most dangerous.

In my primary relationship today, I am able to share openly about my life experiences, and I continue to learn through the sharing. The woman I am involved with knows this story I have written. She was also an abused child and has had homosexual experiences. It is difficult to describe how freeing it is to be open, unashamed, and accepting. I couldn't have achieved this had it not been for all the people in my life, most especially my brother Thom. Through his death I have experienced a rebirth.

> Mick's story is relevant to understanding any employee who is facing a life-threatening illness of a family member. Mick's acceptance of his brother enabled him to focus on what was truly important—showing his brother that he loved him and finding peace with him before he died. In such situations, managers who know how to support their employees in times of crises become finer managers. Unfortunately, when it comes to illnesses—such as AIDS—that are charged with issues around sexual orientation, many managers are ill-equipped to manage effectively. Our belief is that in learning to better manage issues of sexual orientation, you will become better able to manage all workplace issues. These issues include AIDS and other life-threatening illnesses and crises.

Volunteer

Nothing in my life prepared me for the day when I came face to face with the reality that my oldest son is gay. The subject was taboo. Let me start by giving you some idea how my attitudes were formed.

I was raised in Oklahoma, the only child of an only child. There were many only children born during the days following the Great Depression. There was nothing particularly unusual about my childhood until my father lost his job when I was six. He was unable to find work which would sustain our small family, so he went to Texas, where he could earn enough to support himself and pay the storage on our furniture. My mother and I stayed in Oklahoma. We moved in with his parents, where we lived for two years. I felt no deprivation whatever. I was the adored only grandchild of the County Sheriff. He and my grandmother lived in a tiny town, where I was a rather large duck in a small puddle.

Mother, on the other hand, found this period of her life almost unbearable. She had no money of her own. The only negative impact this period had on me is that I have a near obsession with financial security. Mother has told me how difficult it was for her to ask for money for even the most personal items. My grandparents loved her as if she were their own, so I'm sure they saw to it that we both had whatever we needed. Nevertheless, Mother felt embarrassed every time she asked for anything. In this day of women's equality (more or less), I find it curious that she did not get a job herself—or at the very least, negotiate an allowance of some sort. She says the thought of going to work never entered her head. Perhaps she was unwilling to consider that she might be there long enough to get a job.

We were reunited as a family after the beginning of World War II when my father was hired at the federal reformatory in El Reno, Oklahoma. The man who moved with us to El Reno was a very different person from the one who had gone to Texas, however. He had gone through a profound experience— he had given his life to Jesus Christ.

While that was an extraordinarily positive experience for him, it was not so for Mother and me. He was consumed with studying the Bible and with sharing his newfound faith— whether the hearer was interested or not. He was absolutely convinced that what he believed about the Bible was the TRUTH, and there was no discussion about the matter. For the record, fathers in the 1940s were pretty much of a similar turn of mind. "I am Father, therefore I am right," was the prevailing attitude.

El Reno was in the heart of the Bible Belt. Nothing was planned for Sunday morning or Wednesday evening by any civic group or school. Those times were reserved for Church.

People who knew my father during this period described him as generous, caring, and a good friend and neighbor—he even coached a Little League baseball team one year, for the little boy who lived next door whose father was away in the service. Yet even in El Reno, Billy Wilder was something of a curiosity. It didn't take long before people knew better than to let the conversation get around to the Bible. Billy just didn't know when to quit.

Given the environment of both my home and my hometown, I intellectually accepted the Christian teachings; emotionally, I kept them at arm's length. I didn't want to be like my father.

As an only child, I spent a great deal of my time with adults. The family across the street were about the age of my grandparents. I enjoyed their company, and spent many evenings playing cards with them. They often invited me to attend out-of-town basketball games with them. One of their sons, Leo, lived in Oklahoma City, and we would frequently stop at his apartment before games. Leo visited his parents frequently, as well. He was usually accompanied by a roommate, who changed from time to time, but every roommate he had was slender and small, and most worked as hairdressers.

When we visited Leo, it never occurred to me to wonder about the fact that there were two men living there and only one double bed. I was so naive I believed people only had sex for procreation, and I thought intercourse was something rather unpleasant one did in order to have a baby. It's hard to believe that a high school student could be so uninformed, but I was not all that unusual in the early 1950s.

As I reflect on those years, it occurs to me that one of the men for whom I worked as a secretary was probably a homosexual, too. No doubt, there were others who crossed my path, but as I was not looking for them, I never saw them.

I graduated from high school and entered Tulsa University on a scholarship. There I met Jane Blackford, the most winsome Christian it has ever been my pleasure to meet—loving, caring, gentle, and warm. She was never pushy or didactic; she simply talked about Jesus intimately and easily. She gave me a very different Christian role model, and I eagerly accepted Christ as my Savior and became involved in Christian groups on campus.

During this period I also met Tex Black. He was a veteran going to Tulsa University on the GI Bill. He was several years older than I, and very good looking. I fell head over heels in love. I had been very careful to date only Christian young men, for I did not want any conflict about religion in my life. Tex was not a Christian, but he went along with the program and that convinced me that he was absolutely sincere, and he was— until we married. We were still picking the rice out of our hair, figuratively speaking, when he announced, "You can forget about that church stuff now. I've got you."

I was devastated. What could I do? I did not believe in divorce; besides I loved him. How could I have gotten myself into this mess? I believed what I wanted to believe, and now I would have to pay the price. I decided that unless Tex became a Christian, I would never have any children. I could not bear the thought of raising my children in a divided home. I was not playing games here; I was absolutely resolved to this course of action. So I went to church by myself every Sunday; I sang in the choir; and I prayed.

Two years later, Tex graduated from Tulsa University and was baptized. I was ecstatic. Within three months, I was also pregnant.

Andy was born in June of 1956, Kevin came along in August of 1959, and Linda in May of 1962. Two adorable redheaded, brown-eyed boys, and a beautiful little blue-eyed blonde completed our "All American Family," as Tex called it.

However, things weren't going too well in our young married lives. Tex struggled in his career. By the time Linda was born, he had worked for six companies, and we had lived in nine houses. Eventually, I had to look at the possibility that my husband might be responsible for this erratic employment pattern. As a loving and faithful wife, I kept blaming other people for this sequence of events. Finally, he changed industries. That did not help. Later, when Linda was seven years old, he started his own business. I went to work in the company to help out.

My father died suddenly in 1967, at the age of sixty. While I had resisted his Bible instruction during my adolescence, as an adult, I relied on him for answers to my spiritual questions. It must have been rather obvious that my relationship with God was somewhat secondhand, because eventually a friend pointed out to me after my father's death that "God doesn't have any grandchildren." I took this comment to heart. I underwent a significant spiritual awakening and I became involved in several Bible studies.

I enjoyed being a full-time wife and mother, and I did not want to work. As soon as we could reasonably afford to hire someone to take my place in Tex's business, I went back home to care for my children. With no day care facilities in 1969, one summer of juggling children and a job was all I could endure.

When Andy was fourteen, I heard through the grapevine that he had told a friend that he thought he was gay. I was absolutely unwilling to accept even the remotest possibility it might be true. I did ask my pastor to talk to Andy. Dr. Pruett agreed, but what he told Andy was, "If you're gay, you'll just have to learn to live with it." I was outraged.

Andy went to high school, became involved with Young Life, Youth for Christ, and Campus Crusade for Christ. His friends were as wholesome and wonderful a group of kids as you can possibly imagine. They studied the Bible together and prayed for each other. I was convinced that any talk of homosexuality was gone for good.

By 1977, the financial pressures and our inability to communicate about things that mattered finally took their toll on our marriage. Tex and I were divorced. I moved into a three-bedroom apartment. In 1978, Andy graduated from Indiana University and came to live with me, and we finally had the conversation that we needed to have—about his sexual orientation.

Our memories of this conversation are so different that it is difficult to believe we could be talking about the same situation. I know that witnesses to an incident recount different details, but the only thing Andy and I agree on is that the word "homosexual" was finally spoken between us. And, that didn't mean I accepted it.

You see, I was firmly into denial. I sent Andy to a psychiatrist, convinced that he could be "cured." What I did not know was that the doctor told Andy he "might" be able to help him if Andy were prepared to do the hardest work of his life. Andy's reaction, I found out later, was to say, "I've been doing the hardest work of my life for nine years, accepting myself as I am. Thanks, but no thanks."

Andy let me continue in my dream world; he didn't know what else to do with me. He moved to San Francisco, and I continued, in spite of San Francisco's reputation as a "gay mecca," to believe that he was "cured." I even told him that his moving to San Francisco for him was like a drunk taking a job as a bartender.

Anita Bryant was in all the newspapers; the issue of homosexuality was on everyone's lips. I would have been in the front row, cheering her on, except for the thought that it was just barely possible she might be talking about my son.

Two years later, after Frank Conaty and I were married, my daughter Linda and I visited Andy for a week, and my fragile sense of well-being was shattered into a million pieces. All Andy's friends were couples, men obviously living together, or at least "involved." I could not pretend any more that Andy was going to get married to a woman and live happily ever after.

That is when my hard work began.

Stage One: I wrote to Andy often. I quoted scripture. I condemned.

Stage Two: I stopped condemning. I started listening. I cried a lot.

Stage Three: I moved to New Hampshire. No one knows my son; maybe now I can begin to talk about him. I made those first tentative efforts to speak the words "My son is gay" and I was astonished at the results. It was as if God handpicked every person I opened up to. In every instance, the response was, I have a gay brother or uncle, sister or some other relative. It was incredible. It was as if every person in the world must be related to someone gay.

Stage Four: I met Andy's friends. I find out they were likeable people. Some were outrageous. Some were shy. Some were talented. I was surprised that I genuinely liked them.

This was a long, slow, painful process. There were fits and starts along the way. I listened to a gay Christian talk about his life and heard him debate a member of the Moral Majority. That was a shock. I listened to a scientist make a case for nature, not nurture, as the cause of homosexuality. I began to put away my overwhelming guilt.

The AIDS crisis began. I was terrified that my son would die. His friends began to get sick. They began to die. When the first one was dying, his mother visited him and had to deal with the overwhelming truths that her son was dying and that he was gay. I suffered for her. I tried to imagine what I would do if Andy contracted AIDS. Realistically, I couldn't expect to go to California and stay for an extended period of time. It did not seem like a good option for Andy to come to where I lived, leaving all that would be familiar, including his friends, behind. It seemed to me that the next best thing I could do would be to take care of some other mother's son who needed me. So I began to look for an AIDS agency with which to become involved.

I was still living in New Hampshire, and the epidemic was in its infancy. Support systems were barely beginning. So it was not until I moved to central Massachusetts that I found a place where I could be of use. Early in 1987, I volunteered with AIDS Project–Worcester (APW). I answered phones, surveyed funeral homes, staffed the information line, and tried to make myself useful. But I wanted to be involved with the patients. Eventually APW started training buddies. I was in the first group. It was a wonderful experience. We were a very eclectic group. Gay men, straight men, lesbians, straight women, mothers, fathers, people with no children, ranging in age from late twenties to early sixties. We met twice a month for mutual support. We helped each other when our clients became difficult, when they lost their jobs, when they had to apply for Social Security or welfare, when they fought off opportunistic infections—and when they died. Even though that original group has drifted off in many directions, we developed such a strong bond that I still feel very close to each one of those people.

Ultimately, I dived back into the Scripture and studied the passages which dealt with homosexuality in the original Greek and Hebrew. Andy and I even coauthored a book about our experiences. I had to confront the Scripture before I could satisfactorily complete our book. I still believe that the Bible is the Word of God. I still believe that Jesus Christ is God the Son, the second person of the Trinity. I still believe that the only way to become a child of God is through the death and resurrection of Jesus Christ.

However, I now believe that God is grieved when Christians deny His grace to any human being. My Bible says, "Whosoever will may come." It does not say, "unless they're gay." My Bible says, "Come unto me, all ye who labor and are heavy laden, and I will give you rest." It does not say, "except the homosexuals."

I believe that God's grace is sufficient for everyone who ever lived. I have no right, nor does anyone else, to tell someone they are too evil for God's grace. That is not what my Bible teaches me.

Today I am the Buddy Coordinator at AIDS Project–Worcester. I am working with my third AIDS client—a wonderful woman who is an inspiration to all who know her. It grieves her that she is treated differently from other AIDS patients. She is viewed as an "innocent victim" because she was infected when a medical technician stuck her in the hand with a needle that had just been used to draw blood from an AIDS patient. She says it shouldn't matter how a person becomes infected. It should only matter that he or she is sick.

In June of 1992 I was sworn in on Governor Weld's Commission on Gay and Lesbian Youth in the Commonwealth of Massachusetts. It is the first of its kind in the nation. It has been a real privilege to work with the twenty-six other people on this Commission. We hope that what we are doing will pave the way for understanding and compassion toward gay and lesbian young people all over the nation. Governor Weld was moved to create this commission by a federal report which showed that over thirty percent of teenage suicides are related to gay issues. If we use the generally accepted figure that ten percent of the population is gay, that means gay young people are killing themselves three times as often as straight young people. If we use the religious right's figure that one to two percent of the population is gay, those statistics are even more alarming.

I am convinced that one of the most important factors leading to the low self-image and the problems that lead to suicide among this population is the attitude of a great many Christians in this country. Our gay children are told they are evil, depraved, unacceptable, disgraceful, morally degenerate, and twisted.

It is all very well to talk about loving the sinner and hating the sin, but to gays and lesbians everywhere, those words are hollow. They feel hated. And if the people who are homophobic and antigay would be honest with themselves, they would acknowledge that they do hate gays and lesbians.

I believe education is the answer. People like me must come forward and say, "I have a gay son. He's a fine man. I love him very much." The most valuable contribution I can make in the battle for understanding is my own vulnerability. I am not afraid or ashamed any more. I do not care what other people think. I am secure in the love of God for me and for my son. I had every homophobic hang-up you can possibly imagine, and it took a lot of work and a long time for me to get to where I am today. If I can do it, anyone can.

> Luann's story reveals how even those with strongly held negative positions on homosexuality can come to a place of acceptance and support. And, like Art Moreno's story, Luann's shows how much energy and effort go into "coming out" as a parent of a gay person. She spent most of her life as a fundamentalist, judging and condemning. But, her desire to know her son caused her to listen and to communicate, which eventually led her to a place of acceptance and an active role in support of gay rights as a member of the Governor of Massachuetts's Task Force on Gay and Lesbian Youth. It also brought her and her son together. Luann's progression through the various stages of acceptance provides an important example of just how far one can move.

Finding Resources

7

The Workplace and Beyond

This guide provides an array of resources to help you effectively manage gay, lesbian, and bisexual workplace issues and to keep abreast of the latest in how to create a supportive and productive environment for today's diverse workforce.

We encourage you to fully use the resources in this chapter. This may involve taking new risks and stretching yourself. For example, you may feel embarrassed about calling a gay group on the phone. However, by doing so, you increase the likelihood of feeling more comfortable when you next talk with a gay colleague or employee. You also open yourself to the possibility of discovering new information to foster an all-inclusive workplace.

The resources in this chapter include:

>> A list of consultants who specialize in gay, lesbian, and bisexual issues in the workplace.

>> A list of gay and lesbian business organizations throughout the English-speaking world.

>> A sampling of company-sponsored employee groups that support gay, lesbian, and bisexual employers.

>> A list of community organizations throughout the English-speaking world. While these groups exist to provide information to the local gay community, most are happy to

serve the business community as well.

>> A list of additional organizations that may be of help in answering legal questions, developing marketing strategies, and addressing investment and other concerns related to the gay community and gay employees.

>> An index of recent news articles on such topics as gay rights and the workplace, being open in the workplace, and equal benefits.

>> A list of books and articles on sexual orientation in the workplace, including academic and applied research studies.

>> A list of related books on such topics as gay and lesbian history, physical and mental health issues, gay and lesbian parenting, aging, and AIDS.

These resources will help you to stay current and effectively manage these workplace issues.

CONSULTANTS

The following organizations and individuals offer consulting services, deliver speeches, and develop and provide training on gay, lesbian, and bisexual workplace issues. In selecting consultants, we suggest that you focus on four specific criteria:

1 the prior experience of the consultants,
2 their reputation,
3 the demonstrated value of their services,
4 evidence of adherence to professional standards and competencies.

You can assess these criteria by contacting previous clients and others who have made use of the consultant's services. You can further assess criterion three by reviewing the consultant's proposed services and the perceived value to you. Criterion four can be assessed by asking consultants to provide evidence of adherence to such criteria and by noting the consultant's association with professional organizations.

Bob Powers & Associates, Inc.
142 Ord St.
San Francisco, CA 94114
(415) 252-1697

Kaplan, Lucas & Associates
221 S. 12th St.
Philadelphia, PA 19107
(215) 923-1203

Brian McNaught
111 W 67th St. #40A
New York, NY 10023
(212) 336-5640

Ed Mickens
P.O. Box 2079
New York, NY 10108
(212) 769-2384

Kathy Obear
The Human Advantage
6 University Dr., Suite 125
Amherst, MA 01002
(413) 582-3515

Gretchen A. Groth, Ph.D.
G&L Consultants
2525 Grape St.
Denver, CO 80207
(303) 355-2767

George Simons International
740 Front St.
Santa Cruz, CA 95060
(408) 425-9608

Ellen Abell
P.O. Box 271545
Fort Collins, CO 80527-1545
(303) 225-2371

Liz Winfield/Sue Spielman
Common Ground, Inc.
10 Home Ave.
Natick, MA 01766
(508) 651-1476

GAY, LESBIAN, AND BISEXUAL BUSINESS ORGANIZATIONS

Many major urban areas have assocations for gay and lesbian business professionals such as the Golden Gate Business Association of San Francisco and the Greater Seattle Business Association. In addition to providing networking and social activities for their members, these associations also provide educational activities for businesses and corporations. Often they are willing to provide speakers. Like many gay groups, these organizations are growing rapidly. To determine if there is a business organization in your area, check the following list or contact the community organization nearest you (see the following section on community organizations).

United States
Arizona

Camelback Business and Professional Association
P.O. Box 2097
Phoenix, AZ 85001
(602) 225-8444

Valley Career Women
Phoenix, AZ 85001
(602) 493-8759

California

Bay Area Career Women
55 New Montgomery Street, Suite 60
San Francisco, CA 94105
(415) 495-5393

Central California Alliance
P.O. Box 16422
Fresno, CA 93755
(209) 222-7512

Central Coast Business and Professional Association
1694 Newport Avenue
Grover Beach, CA 93433
(805) 489-9597

Desert Business Association
P.O. Box 773
Palm Springs, CA 92263
(619) 324-0178

East Bay Business and Professional Alliance
P.O. Box 20980
Oakland, CA 94620
(510) 287-2571

Gold Coast Business and Professional Association
P.O. Box 7336
Ventura, CA 93006
(805) 388-1545

Golden Gate Business Association, Inc.
1550 California Street, Suite 5L
San Francisco, CA 94109
(800) 303-GGBA Fax (415) 441-1123

Greater San Diego Business Association
P.O. Box 33848
San Diego, CA 92163
(619) 296-4543

Greater Santa Barbara Community Association
P.O. Box 90907
Santa Barbara, CA 93190
(805) 568-3995

Los Angeles Business and Professional Association
P.O. Box 69982
West Hollywood, CA 90069
(213) 896-1444

Orange County Business and Professional Association
P.O. Box 698
Laguna Beach, CA 92652
(714) 240-2035

San Diego Career Women
P.O. Box 880384
San Diego, CA 92168
(619) 552-0650

Southern California Women for Understanding
Los Angeles, CA
(909) 686-5003

Valley Business Alliance
P.O. Box 57555
Sherman Oaks, CA 91413
(808) 982-2650

Colorado
Colorado Business Council
432 S. Broadway
Denver, CO 80209
(303) 595-8042

Rocky Mountain Career Women
P.O. Box 18156
Denver, CO 80218

Florida

Key West Business Guild
P.O. Box 1208
Key West, FL 33041
(305) 294-4603

South Beach Business Guild
718 Lincoln Rd.
Miami Beach, FL 33139
(305) 234-7224

Tampa Bay Business Guild
1222 S. Dale Mabry #656
Tampa, FL 33629
(813) 237-3751

Georgia

Atlanta Executive Network
P.O. Box 77267
Atlanta, GA 30357-1267
(404) 814-1418

Illinois

Chicago Professional Networking Association
Chicago, IL
(312) 935-4561

Kansas

Wichita Business and Professional League
P.O. Box 698
Wichita, KS 67201

Louisiana
>   Gay and Lesbian Business and Professional Association
>   940 Royal #350
>   New Orleans, LA 70116
>   (504) 271-0631

Massachusetts
>   Greater Boston Business Council
>   P.O. Box 1059
>   Boston, MA 02117-1059
>   (617) 236-4222

Michigan
>   Motor City Business Forum
>   29555 N. Western Highway, Suite 516
>   Southfield, MI 48244
>   (810) 546-9347

Missouri
>   St. Louis Business Guild
>   P.O. Box 16822
>   St Louis, MO 63105
>   (no phone)

Nevada
>   Lambda Business Association
>   1801 E. Tropicana #9
>   Las Vegas, NV 89119
>   (702) 593-2875

New Mexico
>   Duke City Business and Professional Association
>   P.O. Box 27207
>   Albuquerque, NM 97125
>   (505) 243-6767

New York
> Gay and Lesbian Business and Professional Guild
> P.O. Box 8392
> White Plains, NY 10602-8392
> (914) 428-8590
>
> Stonewall Business Association
> 27 Peckslip
> New York, NY 10038
> (212) 679-1764
>
> Network of Business and Professional Organizations
> 1416 Third Ave.
> New York, NY 10028
> (212) 517-0771

Ohio
> Queen City Careers Association
> Cincinatti, OH
> (513) 381-5640
>
> The Network
> Cleveland, OH
> (216) 932-2813

Oregon
> Portland Area Business Association
> P.O. Box 6344
> Portland, OR 97228
> (503) 224-2222

Pennsylvania
> Greater Philadelphia Professional Network
> Philadelphia, PA
> (215) 336-9676
>
> Greater Pittsburgh Professional Men's Socicty
> Pittsburgh, PA
> (412) 231-5530

South Carolina
>South Carolina Gay and Lesbian Business Guild
>SCGLBG
>P.O. Box 7913
>Columbia, SC 29202–7913
>(803) 771-7713

Texas
>Stonewall Professional League
>P.O. Box 191343
>Dallas, TX 75219
>(214) 526-6216

Washington
>Greater Seattle Business Association
>2033 6th Avenue #804
>Seattle, WA 98121
>(206) 443-4722

Wisconsin
>Cream City Business Association
>7200 W. Center St.
>Milwaukee, WI 53210
>(no phone)

Australia
>Free Business Association
>P.O. Box 18
>Paddington
>Brisbane QLD 4064

Canada
British Columbia
>Greater Vancouver Business Association
>204-1810 Alberni
>Vancouver, BC V6G 1B3
>(604) 689–5107

Ontario
>   The Fraternity
>   Toronto, ONT
>   (416) 920-2389

British Columbia
>   Gazebo Connection
>   810 W. Broadway #382
>   Vancouver, B.C.
>   (604) 438-5442

New Zealand
>   Gay Auckland Business Association (GABA)
>   P.O. Box 3092
>   Auckland
>   (09) 376-3329

>   Lesbian and Gay Rights Resource Center
>   P.O. Box 11-695
>   Wellington
>   (04) 474-3000 ext 8754

United Kingdom
>   Gay Business Association
>   BMCGBA
>   London, WCIN 3XX
>   (081) 985-9700

>   Northwest Gay Business Association
>   P.O. Box 20
>   Manchester, M60 1Q4

COMPANY-SPONSORED GROUPS

In addition to business associations, hundreds of companies like Boeing, Levi Strauss, Lotus, U.S. West, TimeWarner, and Digital Equipment have company-sponsored gay and lesbian employee groups that provide resources within their organizations and often share information with other companies. Many federal government organizations like the I.R.S. and the Department of Agriculture have similar associations often called GLOBE (Gay, Lesbian or Bisexual Employees of the Federal Government). If you wish to start a group in your company, contact the National Gay and Lesbian Task Force (NGLTF) Workplace Project at (202) 332-6483. If you would like to speak to employees who are a part of such groups, contact one of the following. Most will be happy to help you.

Sample Employee Organizations

AT&T LEAGUE
Hotline (407) 662-3515
TTD Hotline (800) 855-2880

AT&T LEAGUE National Cochairs
John Klenert
8403 Colesville Rd. Rm. 12SB36
Silver Spring, MD 20910-3314
(301) 608-4594

Margaret Burd
11900 N. Pecos St. Rm. 30H-0181
Denver, CO 80234-2703
(303) 538-4430

Federal GLOBE
Leonard Hirsch, Chair
P.O. Box 45237
Washington, D.C. 20026-5237
(202) 986-1101

Apple LAMBDA
20525 Mariani Avenue
Cupertino, CA 95014

BEAGLES
Boeing Employee Association of Gays and Lesbians
The Boeing Company
P.O. Box 1733
Renton, WA 98057

EAGLE (Omaha)
Gay and Lesbian Organization of U.S. West
1314 Douglas, 8th Floor
Omaha, NE 68102

EAGLE (Spokane)
Gay and Lesbian Organization of U.S. West
501 W. 2nd Avenue, Room 201
Spokane, WA 99204

GALAXE
Gay and Lesbian Association of Xerox
P.O. Box 25382
Rochester, NY 14625-0382

Gay and Lesbian Employees of the Red Cross
1197 N. Decatur Rd. NE
Atlanta, GA 30306-2362

Gay and Lesbian Medical Association
2940 16th Street #105
San Francisco, CA 94103

Gay and Lesbian United Airlines Employees Coalition
2261 Market St., Suite 293
San Francisco, CA 94103

Gay, Lesbian and Bisexual Employees of Ameritech
P.O. Box 14308
Chicago, IL 60614

Gay Officers Action League
P.O. Box 2038
Canal Street Station
New York, NY 10013

Gay Pilots Association
P.O. Box 1291
Alexandria, VA 22313

Gays and Lesbian in Foreign Affairs
P.O. Box 18774
Washington, DC 20036-8774

GLEAM
Gay, Lesbian and Bisexual Employees at Microsoft
One Microsoft Way, Bldg 1-1
Redmond, Washington 98052-6399

GLOBAL
Gay and Lesbian Organizations Bridging Across the Land
P.O. Box 42406
Philadelphia, PA 19101-2406

IGLOBE
Intel Gay, Lesbian or Bisexual Employees
Intel Corporation
5200 NE Elam-Young Parkway
Mail Stop HF-273
Hillsboro, OR 98107

Walt Disney League and Alliance
500 S. Buena Vista St.
Burbank, CA 91521

COMMUNITY ORGANIZATIONS

Many community organizations throughout the United States and
Canada offer resources that may be useful to you and your
company. These resources include educational and social materials
and information about the local gay community. In addition, these
organizations generally provide referrals for psycho-social support
for gays and heterosexuals dealing with this issue on personal and
professional levels.

The following is a list of nonprofit community organizations. While
their primary mission is to offer services to the lesbian, gay and
bisexual communities most will do their best to provide information
and help to the business community. The list includes organizations
throughout the English-speaking world. In some cases, groups in

certain areas (for safety and other reasons) do not use the words "gay or lesbian" in their name. Instead, they use words related to the gay community such as "Lambda," "Pride," or "Triangle." These community organizations are volunteer groups and, as such, they undergo frequent changes. If your area is not listed, check your local phone directory to see if there is a listing for a gay and lesbian switchboard or a gay, lesbian, or bisexual student organization on a nearby university campus. Many smaller communities and most universities have such organizations. Or call the National Gay and Lesbian Task Force (202-332-6483). They should be able to connect you to the community organization nearest to you.

United States
Alabama

Lambda Resource Center
205 32nd Street, S.
Birmingham, AL 35255
(205) 326-8600

Alaska

Identity, Inc.
P.O. Box 200070
Anchorage, AK 99520
(907) 258-4777

Arizona

Lesbian/Gay Community Line
P.O. Box 16423
Phoenix, AZ 85011
(602) 234-2752

Arkansas

Arkansas Gay and Lesbian Switchboard
P.O. Box 45053
Little Rock, AR 72214
(501) 375-5504
(800) 448-8305 (in AR only)

California
> Gay and Lesbian Community Services Center
> 1625 Schrader
> Los Angeles, CA 90028
> (213) 993-7430 (ask for community outreach)
> Lesbian and Gay Men's Community Center
> P.O. Box 3357
> 3916 Normal Street
> San Diego, CA 92163
> (619) 692-2077 ext. 820 (Common Ground/Outreach Services)

Colorado
> Gay and Lesbian Community Center of Colorado, Inc.
> 1245 E. Colfax #125
> Denver, CO 80218
> (303) 831-6268

Connecticut
> Gay, Lesbian and Bisexual Community Center
> 1841 Broad Street
> Hartford, CT 06114
> (203) 724-5542

Delaware
> Griffin Community Center
> 214 Market St.
> Wilmington, DE 19801
> (no phone)

District of Columbia
> One in Ten
> 1555 Connecticut Ave., NW, Suite 200
> Washington, DC 20036
> (202) 986-1119

Florida

        Gay and Lesbian Community Center
        P.O. Box 4567
        Ft. Lauderdale, FL 33304
        (305) 563-9500

        Gay and Lesbian Community Services of Central Florida
        P.O. Box 533446
        Orlando, FL 32583
        (407) 843-4297

Georgia

        Atlanta Gay Center
        63 12th Street
        Atlanta, GA 30309
        (404) 876-5372

Hawaii

        Gay Community Center
        1820 University Avenue, 2nd Floor
        Honolulu, HI 96801
        (808) 951-7000

Idaho

        The Community Center
        P.O. Box 323
        Boise, ID 83701
        (no phone)

Illinois

        Horizons Community Services, Inc.
        961 W. Montana
        Chicago, IL 60614
        (312) 472-6469

Indiana

    Justice
    P.O. Box 2387
    Indianapolis, IN 46206
    (317) 9201330

Iowa

    Gay and Lesbian Resource Center
    4211 Grand Avenue
    Des Moines, IA 50312
    (515) 281-0634

Kansas

    Gay and Lesbian Services of Kansas
    Box 13 Kansas Union
    University of Kansas
    Lawrence, KS 55045
    (913) 864-3091

Kentucky

    Williams–Nichols Institute
    P.O. Box 4264
    Louisville, KY 40204
    (502) 636-0935

Louisiana

    Lesbian/Gay Community Center
    816 N. Rampart
    New Orleans, LA 70116
    (504) 522-1103

Maine

    Queer Alliance
    88 Winslow Street
    Portland, ME 04103
    (207) 874-6596

Maryland
> Gay and Lesbian Community Center
> 241 W. Chase Street
> Baltimore, MD 21201
> (410) 837-5445

Massachusetts
> Bisexual Community Resource Services
> 95 Berkeley St., Suite 613
> Boston, MA 02116
> (617) 338-9595

Michigan
> Affirmations Lesbian and Gay Community Center
> 195 W. 9 Mile Road, Suite 106
> Ferndale, MI 48220
> (810) 398-7105

Minnesota
> Gay and Lesbian Community Action Council
> 310 E. 38th Street #204
> Minneapolis, MN 55409
> (612) 822-0127

Mississippi
> G.L. Friendly, Inc. Community Center
> 311 Caillavet St.
> Biloxi, MS 39530
> (601) 435-2398

Missouri
> Gay Services Network
> P.O. Box 32592
> Kansas City, MO 64111
> (816) 931-4470

Challenge Metro
P.O. Box 23227
St. Louis, MO 63156
(314) 367-0084

Montana
Lambda Alliance of Bisexuals, Lesbians and Gay Men
(406) 994-4551

Nebraska
Angle Gay/Lesbian Information and Referral Line
P.O. Box 8343
Omaha, NE 68108
(402) 558-5303

Nevada
Gay and Lesbian Community Center of Las Vegas
P.O. Box 60301
Las Vegas, NV 89160
(702) 733-9800

New Hampshire
Gay Info Line
26 S. Main St. Box 181
Concord, NH 03301
(603) 224-1686

New Jersey
New Jersey Lesbian and Gay Coalition
P.O. Box 1431
New Brunswick, NJ 08903
(908) 828-6772

New Mexico
Common Bond Gay and Lesbian Information
P.O. Box 26836
Albuquerque, NM 87125
(505) 266-8041

New York
>Lesbian and Gay Community Center
>208 W. 13th Street
>New York, NY 10011
>(212) 620-7310

North Carolina
>Our Own Place
>P.O. Box 11732
>Durham, NC 27703
>(919) 821-0055 (Gay/Lesbian Helpline of Wake County)

North Dakota
>Prairie Lesbian/Gay Community
>P.O. Box 83
>Moorhead, ND 56561
>(701) 237-0556

>University Gay/Lesbian Community
>Box 8055
>University Station
>Grand Forks, ND 58202
>(701) 777-4321

Ohio
>Greater Cincinnati Gay/Lesbian Center
>P.O. Box 19518
>Cincinnati, OH 45219
>(513) 651-0040

>Stonewall Community Center
>P.O. Box 10814
>47 W. 5th Avenue
>Columbus, OH 43201
>(614) 299-7764

Lesbian and Gay Community Center of Greater Cleveland
1418 W. 29th
Cleveland, OH 44113
(216) 522-1999

Oklahoma
Oasis Community Center
2135 NW 39th Street
Oklahoma City, OK 73112
(405) 525-2437

Oregon
Oregon Gay and Lesbian Cultural
Resource Center Task Force
P.O. Box 6012
Portland, OR 97228
(503) 283-1811 (NGLTF Task Force)

Pennsylvania
Gay and Lesbian Community Center of Pittsburgh
P.O. Box 5441
2214 E. Carson Street
Pittsburgh, PA 15206
(412) 422-0114

Puerto Rico
Coalicion Puertorriquena de Lesbianas y Homosexuales
Apartado 1003
Estacion Viejo San Juan
San Juan, PR 00902-1003
(no phone)

Rhode Island
Gay/Lesbian Hotline of Rhode Island
P.O. Box 5671
Providence, RI 02903
(401) 751-3322

Lesbian/Gay & Bisexual Alliance
P.O. Box 1930
SAO Brown University
Providence, RI 02912
(401) 863-3062

Network of Rhode Island
P.O. Box 1474
Pawtucket, RI 02862-1474

Rhode Island Alliance for Lesbian, Gay and Bisexual Civil
Rights
P.O. Box 5558
Weybosset Hill Stn.
Providence, RI 02903

South Carolina
South Carolina Gay and Lesbian Pride Movement, Inc.
1108 Woodrow St.
Columbia, SC 29211
(803) 771-7713

South Dakota
The Coalition
P.O. Box 89803
Sioux Falls, SD 89803
(605) 333-0603

Tennessee
Memphis Gay and Lesbian Community Center
1486 Madison Avenue
Memphis, TN 38104
(901) 726-5790

Texas
Gay/Lesbian Community Alliance
2701 Reagan
Dallas, TX 75219
(214) 528-4233

Utah
>Utah Stonewall Center
>770 South 300 West
>Salt Lake City, UT 84101
>(801) 539-8800

Vermont
>Vermont Coalition of Lesbians and Gay Men
>P.O. Box 1125
>Montpelier, VT 05602

Virginia
>Triangle Services Center
>P.O. Box 11471
>Norfolk, VA 23517
>(no phone)
>also see D.C. listing

Washington
>Seattle Commission on Gays and Lesbians
>Office of Women's Rights
>700 Third Ave., Suite 220
>Seattle, WA 98104
>(206) 684-0390

West Virginia
>West Virginia Coalition for Lesbian and Gay Rights
>P.O. Box 11033
>Charleston, WV 25339
>(304) 965-3187

Wisconsin
>The United
>P.O. Box 310
>Madison, WI 53701
>(608) 255-4297

Wyoming
     United Gays/Lesbians of Wyoming
     P.O. Box 2037
     Laramie, WY 82070
     (307) 632-5362

Australia
Adelaide
     Gay and Lesbian Community Library
     Darling House
     64 Fullerton Street
     Norwood
     South Australia 5067
     (no phone)

Albury
     Central Network
     P.O. Box 1738
     Albury
     New South Wales 2640
     (060) 53-2844

Canberra
     Gayline
     G.P.O. Box 229
     Canberra
     Australian Capital Territory 2601
     (062) 247-2726

Hobart
     Tasmanian Gay and Lesbian Rights Group
     G.P.O. Box 1773
     Hobart
     Tasmania 7000
     (002) 243-556

Launceston
> Northern Link
> P.O. Box 801
> Launceston
> Tasmania 7000
> (002) 34-3254

Melbourne
> ALSO Foundation
> 35 Cata Street
> Pahran
> Victoria
> (no phone)

Newcastle
> Newcastle Gay and Lesbian Information Service
> P.O. Box 425
> Newcastle
> New South Wales 2300
> (049) 29-3464

Perth
> Gay and Lesbian Equality
> P.O. Box 912
> Perth
> Western Australia 6005
> (no phone)

Sandy Bay
> Gay and Lesbian Community Centre
> P.O. Box 818
> Sandy Bay
> Tasmania 7005
> 297-649

Sydney
>Gay and Lesbians Rights Lobby
>P.O. Box 9
>Darlinghurst
>Sydney
>New South Wales 2010
>(02) 360-6650

>Pride: The Sydney Lesbian and Gay Community Cetre Ltd.
>P.O. Box 7
>Darlinghurst
>New South Wales
>(no phone)

>Sydney Gay and Lesbian Association
>P.O. Box 394
>Darlinghurst
>New South Wales 2010
>(02) 264-6233

Canada
Alberta
>Gay and Lesbian Community Center of Edmonton
>P.O. Box 1852
>Edmonton, AB TJ5 2P2
>(403) 488-3234

British Columbia
>Gay and Lesbian Centre
>1170 Bute Street
>Vancouver, BC V6E 1Z6
>(604) 684-6869

Manitoba
>Gay and Lesbian Resource Center
>P.O. Box 1661
>Winnipeg, MB R3C 2Z6
>(204) 284-5208

Winnipeg
    Gay and Lesbian Resource Centre
    1-222 Osborne Street S.
    Winnipeg
    (204) 284-5208

Ontario
    Coalition for Lesbian and Gay Rights in Ontario
    P.O. Box 822 Station A
    Toronto, ON M5W 1G3
    (416) 533-6824

Toronto
    Khush
    519 Church Street
    P.O. Box 6172
    Stn A M5W 1P6
    Toronto
    (no phone)

Ottawa
    Centre 318
    318 Lisgar St.
    Ottawa
    (613) 233-0152

    Pink Triangle Services
    71 Bank Street #203
    Ottawa
    (613) 563-4818

Quebec
    Centre Communautaire des Gaies et Lesbiennes Montreal
    CP 476 Succ. C
    Montreal, QC H2L 4K4
    (514) 990-1414

Israel
Haifa
>Society for the Protection of Personal Rights (SPPR)
>1 Carlozorof St.
>Haifa
>(04) 672-665

Tel Aviv
>Society for the Protection of Personal Rights (SPPR)
>28 Nahmani St.
>Tel Aviv
>(03) 293681

New Zealand
Auckland
>Auckland Gay and Lesbian Community Centre
>44–46 Ponsonby Rd.
>1st flr
>Auckland
>(09) 302-0590

Christchurch
>Gaylink
>P.O. Box 25-165
>Christchurch
>(03) 379-9493

Napier
>Gay Community Trust/Centre
>Parker Chamers
>Herschell Street
>P.O. Box 659, 2nd flr
>Napier
>(06) 835-7190

Wellington
>   Lesbian and Gay Archives of New Zealand
>   P.O. Box 11695
>   Manners Street
>   Wellington
>   (04) 474-3000

South Africa
Johannesburg
>   Gay and Lesbian Hotline
>   Johannesburg
>   (011) 643-2311

Pretoria
>   Gay Community Centre
>   Schoemann St.
>   Pretoria, SA
>   (012) 325-6664

United Kingdom
England
>   Campaign for Homosexual Equality (CHE)
>   38 Mount Pleasant
>   London WC1X OAP
>   (0171) 833 39 12
>
>   Stonewall Lobby Group
>   2 Greycoat Place
>   London SW1P 1SB
>   222 90 07

Ireland
>   Hirschfield Center
>   10 Fownes St.
>   Dublin
>   (01) 671 09 39

NIGRA (Northern Ireland Gay Rights Association)
P.O. Box 44
8 Long Street
Belfast BT1 1SH
66 41 11

Scotland
Lesbian and Gay Community Centre
58A Broughton Street
Edinburgh EH1 3SA
(031) 558 12 79

Glasgow Lesbian and Gay Centre Project
P.O. Box 463
Glasgow G12 8PN
221 83 72

Wales
CYLCH
c/o Intervol
Shand Hose
2 Fitzalan Pl.
Wales
34 01 01

OTHER RESOURCES

There are a host of other resources that provide useful information
to corporations. A brief description of what they do follows each
listing.

National Gay/Lesbian Task Force
2320 17th Street N.W.
Washington DC 20009
(202) 332-6483
Surveys and reports on Fortune 1000 companies and provides a
list of relevant publications. Call to receive list.

Human Rights Campaign Fund
P.O. Box 1396
Washington, DC 20013
(202) 628-4160

Sponsors workplace panel discussions, helps people come out in the workplace, and encourages dialogue around these issues.

Overlooked Opinions
3162 N. Broadway
Chicago, IL 60657
(312) 929-9600

Marketing Survey Organization that monitors over 50,000 gay and lesbian households.

Progressive Assets Management
1814 Franklin Street
Oakland, CA
(510) 834-3722

Investment firm that monitors corporate treatment of gays and lesbians.

ACLU
Lesbian and Gay Rights Project
132 W. 43rd Street
New York, NY 10036
(212) 944-9800

Provides legal resources on workplace issues.

Life Management: The Lesbian and Gay Information Service
Contact: Brian N. Kleis, M.D.
P.O. Box 50516
Palo Alto, CA 94303
(415) 324-1310

Provides a variety of life management services for gay, lesbian, and bisexual individuals. This firm works with corporations in offering their employees such services.

Hollywood Supports
6430 Sunset Boulevard, Suite 102
Los Angeles, CA 90028
(213) 962-3118

An entertainment industry project that offers seminars and information.

Positive Resource: A Program of The Life Center
1675 California Street
San Francisco, CA 94109
(415) 928-1448

Offers work referrals for people living with HIV.

The NAMES Project Foundation
310 Townsend St., Suite 310
San Francisco, CA 94107
(415) 882-5500

Sponsors the AIDS Memorial Quilt

Parents and Friends of Lesbians and Gays (P–FLAG)
1101 14th Street 10th Floor
Washington, DC 20005
(202) 638-4200

While not directly linked to business, this organization offers support to parents and friends of lesbians and gays. There are P–Flag chapters in most cities and many rural areas. The national organization will refer you to the P-FLAG group nearest you.

NEWS ARTICLES

The following is a collection (from electronic databases and other sources) of articles in major news media that relate to the issue of gays and lesbians in the workplace. You may find some of the information in these articles useful in preparing internal reports and, possibly, for external press releases, etc.

The articles are divided by issue:

>> Gay Rights and the Workplace
>> Being Open in the Workplace

>> Equal Benefits
>> Company Reputation and Marketing

You will note that the articles generally cover the period after 1991 because very little was published in the popular media about gay issues in the workplace prior to that time.

Index to News Articles

Gay Rights and the Workplace

"Gay Staffers Protected by Majority of Congressional Employers." *New York Native*, April 24, 1995. (No author.)

"Survey Finds More Firms Banning Anti-Gay Bias." *San Francisco Chronicle*, June 21, 1994. David Tuller.

"Gay Rights May Be Social Issue of 1990s." *Christian Science Monitor*, February 11, 1993. Brad Knickerbocker.

"A Lose-Lose Veto." *U.S. News & World Report*, October 14, 1991. Staff.

Being Open in the Workplace

"A Quiet Liberation for Gay and Lesbian Employees." *New York Times*, June 13, 1993. Barbara Presley Noble.

"Disruption Rare as Gays Have Been Integrated." *Los Angeles Times*, January 30, 1993. Alan C. Miller.

"Firms Step Up Hiring of Gay and Lesbian Lawyers." *New York Times*, February 7, 1992. Jana Eisinger.

"Gay In Corporate America." *Fortune*, December 16, 1991. Thomas A. Stewart.

"Good For Business: Why Companies are Bringing Gay Rights Out of the Closet." *Working Woman Magazine*, December 1991. Meryl Davids.

"Managing: Gay Rights, Issue of the 90s." *New York Times*, April 28, 1991. Claudia H. Deutsch.

"Bob Powers: An Unconventional Success Story." *Training*, August 1986. Dale Feuer.

Offering Equal Benefits

"A New Openness to Benefits." *New York Times*, June 13, 1993. Barbara Presley Noble.

"More Employers Extend Benefits to Gay Partners." *Wall Street*

Journal, March 6, 1992. Sue Shellenbarger.
"A Cutting-Edge Issue: Benefits." *Fortune,* December 16, 1991. Thomas A. Stewart.
"Lotus Offers Benefits for Homosexual Pairs." *New York Times,* Sept. 7, 1991. Associated Press.

Company Reputation and Marketing
"Firms Rated for Sexual Politics." *San Francisco Examiner,* September 9, 1993. Kathleen Sullivan.
"With Varying Degrees of Openness, More Companies Lure Gay Dollars." *New York Times,* March 2, 1992. Georgia Dullea.
"Top Ten." *The Advocate*, June 16, 1992. Paul Katzoff.

BOOKS AND ARTICLES ON SEXUAL ORIENTATION IN THE WORKPLACE

To date, relatively little research has been conducted on issues relating to gays, lesbians, and bisexuals in the workplace. However, the interest in this area seems to be accelerating the pace at which research is being done, and a significant increase in the number of academic and research articles might be expected in the near future.

The following articles and books were found using electronic databases, and through conversations with various journal editors and others.

Books
Diamant, L. (1993). *Homosexual Issues in the Workplace.* New York: Taylor & Francis.
Ellis, A. L., & Riggle, E. D. (Forthcoming). *Sexual Identity Issues in the Work Place.* Binghampton, New York: Haworth Press.
Woods, J., & Lucas, J. (1993). *The Corporate Closet.* New York: The Free Press.
Zuckerman, A.J. and G.F. Simons (1994). *Sexual Orientation in the Workplace.* Santa Cruz, CA: International Partners Press.

Articles
Anderson, C. W., & Smith, H. R. (1993). "Stigma and Honor: Gay, Lesbian and Bisexual People in the U. S. Military." In L.

Diamant (ed.), *Homosexual Issues in the Workplace.* (pp. 65–89). New York: Taylor & Francis.

Earnshaw, J. (1991). "Homosexuals and Transsexuals at Work: Legal Issues." In M. J. Davidson & J. Earnshaw (eds.), *Vulnerable Workers: Psychosocial and Legal Issues.* (pp. 241–257). Chichester, England: John Wiley & Sons.

Elliott, J. E. (1993). "Lesbian and Gay Concerns in Career Development." In L. Diamant (ed.), *Homosexual Issues in the Workplace.* (pp. 25–43). New York: Taylor & Francis.

Ellis, A. L., & Riggle E. D. (Forthcoming). "The Relation of Job Satisfaction and Degree of Openness About One's Sexual Orientation for Lesbians and Gay Men. *Journal of Homosexuality.*

Ellis, A. L., & Vasseur, R. B. (1993). "The Impact of Interpersonal Exposure to Gays and Lesbians on Employment Interviewing Strategy. *Journal of Homosexuality* 25, 31–46.

Etringer, B. D., Hillerbrand, E., & Hetherington, C. (1990). "The Influence of Sexual Orientation on Career Decision-Making: A Research Note. *Journal of Homosexuality,* 19(4), 103–111.

Gonsiorek, J. C. (1993). "Threat, Stress, and Adjustment: Mental Health and the Workplace for Gay and Lesbian Individuals." In L. Diamant (ed.), *Homosexual Issues in the Workplace.* (pp. 243–264). New York: Taylor & Francis.

Hall, M. (1986). "The Lesbian Corporate Experience." *Journal of Homosexuality* 16, pp. 59–75.

Hedgpeth, J. M. (1980). "Discrimination and the Rights of Gay People." In D. C. Knutson (ed.), *Homosexuality and the Law.* Binghampton, New York: The Haworth Press.

Herek, G. M. (1990). "Gay People and Government Security Clearances: A Social Science Perspective." *American Psychologist,* 45, 1035–1042.

Herek, G. M. (1991, August). "Is Homosexuality Compatible with Military Service? A Review of the Social Science Data." Symposium conducted at American Psychological Association Convention, San Francisco.

Hetherington, C., Hillerbrand, E., & Etringer, B. (1989). "Career Counseling with Gay Men: Issues and Recommendations for Research." *Journal of Counseling and Development,* 67, 452–454.

Hetherington, C., & Orzek, A. (1989). "Career Counseling and Life Planning with Lesbian Women." *Journal of Counseling and Development*, 68, 52–56.

Hickey, J. (June 7, 1993). "Dealing with the Gay Dimension of Diversity." *Human Resource Management News*, 2.

Hunter, N. D., et al. (1992). *The Rights of Lesbians and Gay Men: The Basic ACLU Guide to a Gay Person's Rights*. New York: New Press

Kitzinger, C. (1991). "Lesbians and Gay Men in the Workplace: Psychosocial Issues." In M. J. Davidson & J. Earnsha (Eds.), *Vulnerable Workers: Psychosocial and Legal Issues*. (pp. 223–240). Chichester, England: John Wiley & Sons.

Kronenberger, G. (1991). "Out of the Closet." *Personnel Journal*, 70, 40–44.

Lee, J. A., & Brown, R. G. (1993). "Hiring, Firing, and Promotion." In L. Diamant (ed.), *Homosexual Issues in the Workplace*. (pp 45–62). New York: Taylor & Francis.

Levine, M. P. (1979). "Employment Discrimination Against Gay Men." *International Review of Sociology*, 9, 151–163.

Levine, M. P., & Leonard, R. (1984). "Discrimination Against Lesbians in the Work Force." *Signs: Journal of Women in Culture and Society*, 9, 700–710.

National Gay and Lesbian Task Force Policy Institute (1993, October). *Workplace Issues Project Preliminary Survey of the Fortune 1000 Companies on Issues of Importance to Gays, Lesbians and Bisexuals*. Washington, D.C.: National Gay and Lesbian Task Force.

Powers, B. (November/December 1993). "What It's Like to Be Gay in the Workplace." *Performance & Instruction*, 32.

Schneider, B. (1986). "Coming Out at Work: Bridging the Private/Public Gap." *Work and Occupations*, 13, 463–487.

Sussal, C. M. (1994). "Empowering Gays and Lesbians in the Workplace." *Journal of Gay and Lesbian Social Services*, 1, 89–103.

Whitman, F. J., & Dizon, M. J. (1979). "Occupational Choice and Sexual Orientation in Cross-Cultural Perspective." *International Review of Modern Sociology*, 9, 137–149.

Williamson, A. D. (July-August 1993). "Is This the Right Time to Come Out?" *Harvard Business Review*. 18–27.

Wolfson, E. (1994). *Out on the Job, Out of a Job: A Lawyers Overview of the Employment Rights of Lesbians and Gay Men*. New York: Lambda Legal Defense and Education Fund.

BEYOND THE WORKPLACE: FURTHER READING

Managers who want to deepen their knowledge of the sexual minority community can do so by drawing from the following list of readings.

Gay, Lesbian, and Bisexual Relatives and Friends

The books in this category focus on the concerns of heterosexuals who have a friend or relative who is gay or lesbian and are wondering how best to respond.

Borhek, M. V. (1979). *My Son Eric: A Mother Struggles to Accept Her Gay Son and Discover Herself*. New York: Pilgrim Press.

Borhek, M. V. (1983). *Coming Out to Parents: A Two-Way Survival Guide for Lesbians and Gay Men and Their Parents*. New York: Pilgrim Press.

Clark, D. (1987). *Loving Someone Gay*. Berkeley, CA: Celestial Arts.

Fairchild, B. & Hayward, N. (1979). *Now That You Know: What Every Parent Should Know About Homosexuality*. New York: Harcourt Brace Jovanovich.

Griffin, C. W., Wirth, M. J., & Wirth, A. G. (1986). *Beyond Acceptance: Parents of Lesbians and Gays Talk About Their Experiences*. Engelwood Cliffs, New Jersey: Prentice-Hall.

Gay and Lesbian Parenting

These books offer useful information on gay and lesbian parents.

Barret, R. L., & Robinson, B. E. (1990). *Gay Fathers*. Lexington, MA: Lexington Books.

Bozett, F. W. (1987). *Gay and Lesbian Parents*. New York: Praeger.

Pollack, S., & Vaughn, J. (1987). *Politics of the Heart: A Lesbian Parenting Anthology*. Ithaca, NY: Firebrand Books.

Homosexuality and Religion

The five books in this section offer thorough and careful considerations of the challenge many face in reconciling religious beliefs with homosexuality.

> Boswell, J. (1980). *Christianity, Social Tolerance, and Homosexuality*. Chicago: University of Chicago Press.
> Denman, R. M. (1990). *Let My People In*. New York: William Morrow.
> Hilton, B. (1992). *Can Homophobia be Cured? Wrestling with Questions that Challenge the Church*. Nashville, TN: Abingdon Press.
> McNeil, J. H. (1988). *The Church and the Homosexual*. Boston: Beacon Press.
> Mollenkott, V., & Scanzoni, L. (1978). *Is the Homosexual My Neighbor? Another Christian View*. San Francisco: Harper & Row.

Aging Issues

These books focus on the concerns of aging gay men and lesbians.

> Berger, R. (1982). *Gay and Gray: The Older Homosexual Man*. Boston: Alyson Press.
> Kehoe, M. (1989). *Lesbians Over 60 Speak for Themselves*. Binghamton, NY: Haworth Press.

Coming Out/General Issues

Books on acceptance and the process of coming out are included here.

> Clark, D. (1979). *Living Gay*. Millbrae, CA: Celestial Arts.
> Duberman, M. (1993). *Stonewall*. New York: Dutton.
> Isay, R. (1989). *Being Homosexual: Gay Men and Their Development*. New York: Farrar, Straus, Giroux.
> McNaught, B. (1988). *On Being Gay*. New York: St. Martin's Press.
> Rothblum, E. D., Cole, E. (1989). *Loving Boldly—Lesbianism: Affirming Nontraditional Roles*. Binghamton, NY: Haworth Press.
> Troiden, R. R. (1988). *Gay and Lesbian Identity: A Sociological Analysis*. Dix Hills, NY: General Hall.

Gay and Lesbian History
These are books on the history of the gay community.

Katz, J. N. (1992—revised edition). *Gay American History: Lesbians and Gay Men in the U.S.A.* New York: Meridian.

Liebman, M. (1992). *Coming Out Conservative.* San Francisco: Chronicle Books.

Marcus, E. (1992). *Making History.* New York: St. Martin's Press.

Penelope, J., & Valentine, S. (1990). *Finding the Lesbians: Personal Accounts from Around the World.* Freedom, CA: Crossing Press.

Physical and Mental Health Issues
Boston Lesbian Psychology Collective (1987). *Lesbian Psychologies: Exploration and Challenges.* Urbana: University of Illinois Press.

Delaney, M. & Goldblum, P. (1987). *Strategies for Survival: A Gay Men's Health Manual for the Age of AIDS.* New York: St. Martin's Press.

Hunter, N.D. & Rubenstein, W. B. (1992). *AIDS Agenda: Emerging Issues in Civil Rights.* New York: New Press.

Legal Issues
These are primers on legal concerns and the rights of gays and lesbians.

Hunter, N. D. et al. (1992). *The Rights of Lesbians and Gay Men: The Basic ACLU Guide to a Gay Person's Rights.* New York: New Press.

Rubenstein, W. B. (1993). *Lesbians, Gay Men, and the Law.* New York: New Press.

AIDS in the Workplace
These books deal with AIDS—one focuses specifically on AIDS in the workplace.

Banta, W. F. (1993). *AIDS in the Workplace.* New York: Lexington.

Huber, J. T. (1992). *How to Find Information about AIDS.*

Binghamton, NY: Harrington Park Press.

Land, H. (1992). *A Complete Guide to Psychosocial Intervention*. Milwaukee: FSA Publishers.